Wagner in Thought and Practice

BOOKS BY GEOFFREY SKELTON

Wagner at Bayreuth: Experiment and Tradition
(1965, 2nd revised edn. 1976)

Wieland Wagner:
The Positive Sceptic (1971)

Paul Hindemith: The Man behind the Music
(1975, 2nd impr. 1977)

Richard and Cosima Wagner:
Biography of a Marriage (1982)

as translator

Wagner Writes from Paris
(with Robert L. Jacobs, 1973)

Cosima Wagner's Diaries
(2 vols, 1978 and 1980)

Arden Must Die (libretto Fried/Goehr)

Le Grand Macabre (libretto Meschke/Ligeti)

as contributor

The New Grove Dictionary
of Music and Musicians (on Bayreuth)

The New Grove Dictionary
of Opera (on Bayreuth and the operas of Hindemith)

GEOFFREY SKELTON

Wagner in Thought and Practice

First published in Great Britain 1991
by Lime Tree
an imprint of the Octopus Publishing Group
Michelin House, 81 Fulham Road, London SW3 6RB

Copyright © 1991 by Geoffrey Skelton
The author has asserted his moral rights

A CIP catalogue record for this book is available from
the British Library
ISBN 0 413 45271 9

Typeset by Falcon Typographic Art Ltd,
Edinburgh & London
Printed in Great Britain
by St Edmundsbury Press, Bury St Edmunds, Suffolk

Contents

Acknowledgements

The chapters on *Tannhäuser*, *Parsifal* and the role of the actor-singer are based on features which I wrote for radio, and which were broadcast either by the British Broadcasting Corporation or by Südwestfunk in Germany, two of them by both. The chapter on Bayreuth is a slightly adapted and expanded version of an essay which first appeared under the title 'The Idea of Bayreuth' in *The Wagner Companion*, edited by Peter Burbidge and Richard Sutton and published by Faber and Faber. The three other chapters are new.

The translations from Wagner's works are for the main part my own, made specifically for this book. The extracts from *Cosima Wagner's Diaries* are also in my translation, published in the United States by Harcourt Brace Jovanovich and in the United Kingdom by Collins. When I have made use of translations by others I have indicated the fact in a footnote. These translators are Robert L. Jacobs (*Three Wagner Essays*, Eulenburg Books) and Andrew Porter (*The Ring of the Nibelung*, Faber Music Ltd).

Ends and Means:

Opera and Drama in Thought

In his introduction to *Opera and Drama* (*Oper und Drama*)
Wagner set out in heavy black type the belief that had led
him to write his book: 'The error into which opera as an art
form has fallen is that music, the means of expression, has
been made the end, while the true end, which is drama, has
become the means.'

His attempt, first to validate this assertion and then to
indicate how a true balance might be achieved, took him
some 150,000 words, all of which he wrote in only four
months – a truly phenomenal achievement. He still found
time in the middle of it to write letters to his friends Theodor
Uhlig in Dresden and Franz Liszt in Weimar, reporting
progress. 'You can have no idea of the trouble I am giving
myself,' he wrote to Uhlig in December 1850, 'to call forth
a whole understanding in those who now understand but
half . . . and I also rejoice that I am always coming to
a better understanding myself.' To Liszt also he admitted
that the book was coming more and more to be addressed
to himself rather than to an outside reader. 'I had to clear up
a whole life behind me,' he wrote on 25 November 1850;
'to draw into the light all the things dawning inside me, to
master the reflections that inevitably rose up inside me by
applying their own methods – that is to say, by examining
as closely as possible what they seemed to be suggesting – in
order once again to throw myself with a clear and cheerful

conscience back into the lovely unconsciousness of artistic creation.'

The artistic creation for which the book cleared his mind very soon followed: it was the text of *Der junge Siegfried (Young Siegfried)*, to precede *Siegfrieds Tod (Siegfried's Death)*, the text of which he had written before his banishment from Dresden. This, and the later idea for two further works to form with the two Siegfried dramas *Der Ring des Nibelungen*, so occupied him that he left to Uhlig the task of finding a publisher for *Opera and Drama* and seeing it through the press. On 21 November 1851 he wrote to his friend, who was preparing an article to coincide with the publication: 'The third part is really the most important. But don't forget to lay stress on subject matter – Part Two – as centre and axis of the whole; for *here* is the crucial point: that I consider form only in the light of content. Hitherto it has been treated quite regardless of content.'

Since Wagner himself pointed to this as the starting point of his theoretical considerations, I shall begin my chapter at this point, skipping the first part of *Opera and Drama*, which is a trenchant survey of the development of opera up to his own time. After repeating the maxim regarding ends and means set out at the beginning, he concluded the first part with the ringing declaration that for a composer to imagine that the aims of drama can be satisfied by music alone was nothing short of madness. He then set out to examine the whole nature of drama as a preliminary to establishing the proper role of music within it.

Drama, he stated, evolved from two main sources: medie-val romances that related colourful episodes in the lives of human heroes, and ancient Greek legend. The first of these led via mystery plays to Shakespearean drama, which is episodic and strong in human characterisation; the second via the Greek tragedians to the drama of Racine, tied to the Aristotelian unities of time, place and action, in which actual happenings are related, not depicted. From this – on the whole uncontroversial – basis he went on to consider how these two types of drama developed over the centuries.

The Elizabethan dramatists, culminating in Shakespeare, brought the shapeless pattern of mystery plays into some kind of order by restricting their length and the number of episodes presented. This was done with the object of introducing a direct appeal to the senses into material that in medieval romances and mystery plays had been addressed solely to the imagination. This appeal was conveyed by words. To ensure that these words could be heard, the action must be presented in a confined space, and to ensure that they would be understood, the action must be restricted to the number of hours in which a grip on the audience's attention could be maintained. Wagner wrote: 'A work of art that appeals only to the imagination, such as the written romance, can easily bear with interruptions, since imagination is so capricious that it obeys no laws but those of chance. Something aimed at the senses with the purpose of making a convincing and unerring impression has, in contrast, not only to take into account the nature, capability and limited physical strength of these senses, it must also reveal itself wholly to them, from top to bottom and from beginning to end, if it is not, through sudden interruption or inadequacy of presentation, to find itself once again having to call, for completion of the picture, on that very imagination from which it has just persuaded the senses to turn.'

One aspect of dramatic presentation the Elizabethan dramatists neglected to consider was that of the visual background against which the action was set. By merely using placards to state where the action is taking place and leaving the actual scenery to the imagination, Shakespeare, for all his unique contribution to drama in the depiction of human character, must bear the blame for 'an unparalleled confusion in dramatic art lasting two centuries.'

It was a confusion that Shakespeare's very different French counterpart, Racine, did nothing at all to dispel. The drama of Shakespeare, with its origin in romance, might be said to have arisen out of the common people, a source for which the cultured French had no taste. For his drama Racine turned to the Latin source from which the French language emerged and from the Roman poets back to those of Greece. Like the Romans themselves, he took from Greece not only the dramatic form, but also the subject matter of their dramas. And, since these borrowed French dramas were played in the splendid halls of princely palaces, the question of scenery did not arise: according to the Aristotelian rules as they were understood, one scene must do for all. 'This meant that the action-packed romance, the basic poetic element of medieval and modern life, was virtually excluded, since it would have been quite impossible to present its many-faceted subject matter without frequent changes of scenery . . . French dramatists . . . had to chose subjects that did not need first of all to be condensed by them into a shape fit for dramatic presentation, but only those that had already been so condensed by others.' As a result of this adoption of a content that had nothing to do with the life of its own times, external factors assumed the dominant role, particularly that of declamation, which in time influenced the character of opera as it developed in Italy and France: 'Opera was therefore the premature blossom of an unripe fruit, grown on unnatural, artificial soil.'

Germany, having no indigenous dramatic art, was familiar with both contrasting forms, which led an uneasy existence side by side: the French style in the palaces of the many petty princes, all vying to outdo each other, and the Shakespearean in the towns and villages visited by English strolling players. At both levels the desire eventually arose for a scenic background to satisfy the visual senses, and the consequence in both cases was a serious diminution of the dramatic content: the elaborate machinery installed in the palace theatres to provide a background spectacle diverted attention from the ear to the eye; while the impossibility of providing an authentic background for each of the many short scenes in a Shakespearean play was made an excuse for cuts and adaptations that took away much of their poetic and dramatic effect. Wagner saw no way of rescuing modern drama from the confusion in which it had landed itself both as regards form and content, except by starting again from the very beginning with an examination of the origins and purposes of poetry.

'The human being is a poet in two ways: in perception and in communication,' he wrote. 'The *natural* poetic talent is the ability to draw together phenomena as they present themselves to the senses in an inner picture; the *artistic* talent is to communicate this picture to others.' The brain is actively engaged in registering perceptions and combining them to form new perceptions of even greater scope, and this activity, he went on, we call imagination. It is an unconscious process, and the being who wishes to communicate the pictures in his mind to others must first bring them within himself into a conscious relationship with reality before he can impart them. Nobody can make himself understood by others unless they share his perceptions: some common basis is needed before communication becomes possible. The only dramatic art yet to emerge that appeals effectively to all the senses at once has been that of ancient Greece, and it drew its subject matter from myth.

Wagner's subsequent reflections on the nature and significance of myth turned what had begun, as he stated in his letter to Uhlig of 20 September 1850, as 'rather a long article on modern opera' into a penetrating study of ways of creating a dramatic art that would fully engage all the senses, and through them the emotions, of his audiences. The first paragraph of his chapter on the subject of myth clearly shows how closely, if as yet unconsciously, his thoughts were tied up with *Der Ring des Nibelungen*, which, as I mentioned at the beginning, had not assumed anything like its final shape at the time of writing *Opera and Drama*.

'In myth the common poetic faculty of a people comprehends phenomena only as seen by the eye, not as they really are. The immense variety of phenomena, whose true connection with one another the individual human being is unable at once to grasp, arouses in him a feeling of unrest. To overcome this feeling he searches around for some common connection that he can grasp as a cause of the phenomena. But only intellect, which comprehends phenomena as they really are, can identify the true connection. For the individual who judges phenomena only by the most immediate impressions they make on him, the connection can be nothing more than a product of his fantasy, and the cause to which he ascribes it a stirring within him of poetic imagination. God and gods were the first creations of this poetic imagination: in them the human being discerned the cause underlying all natural phenomena, and involuntarily he identified this cause with his own human character.' A human being wishing to overcome the feeling of unrest that the immense variety of phenomena induces in him is bound to represent its imagined cause in a form that not only shares his outlook, but also bears an outward resemblance to himself. In myth the popular tendency is to reduce all phenomena to condensed forms, which then tend, the clearer they are required to be, more and more to assume human forms, though their true function may be a superhuman or supernatural one. 'Through its capacity of using its powers of imagination to conjure up all conceivable realities in condensed and clearly recognisable shapes, the human race invented myth and thereby became the creator of art . . . Art is nothing other than a fulfilment of the desire to recognise oneself in the representation of an admired or beloved object, to find oneself reflected in external phenomena made understandable through representation. In the object he is presenting the artist tells himself: "This is how you are, this is how you feel and think, and this is how you would act if, free from the arbitrary pressures of real life, you could act in the way you would choose to act." This is how, in myth, the human race depicted God, heroes and finally individual beings.'

Greek tragedy was the artistic realisation of the content and spirit of Greek myth. It was addressed to a people that shared a common outlook, and, following the pattern of myth itself, presented the chosen subject in a concentrated form, avoiding complication through the introduction of subsidiary themes. The unified form Greek tragedy took was contained in the myth on which it was based, and the dramatist had no reason to alter it. Myth is the poetic expression of a common outlook, and Greek tragedy the artistic realisation of that myth.

The medieval romance, with its multiplicity of themes, was the artistic expression of the civilisation that succeeded the classical world. Things were no longer viewed as a whole, but piecemeal. Mythology gave way to history. The myth of the ancient world still played a role in art, but now it was mixed with Christian myth.

In Greek mythology, Wagner maintained, the human being

was the centre of all thought and imagination, but there was a contradiction between the desires of the community and those of the individual. 'In the conflict between those things the individual regarded as good and just, such as the law and the state, and those towards which his urge for happiness and wish for personal freedom were pushing him, the human being was bound finally to see himself as incomprehensible, and his consequent loss of direction was the starting point of Christian mythology. In this the individual human being, seeking peace within himself, saw salvation in placing his faith in the existence of an other-worldly being to whose unfathomable will the law and the state were themselves subservient and therefore powerless.'

Christian myth was built around the figure of a human being who suffered a martyr's death and thus, while acknowledging the outer authority of the state by consenting to it, nullified that authority by demonstrating the existence in the individual of a higher necessity – to find redemption in God. Death and the promise of an afterlife were the elements of the Christian myth that held the strongest appeal to the emotions.

The third mythological source influencing artistic creation in modern times was the Germanic saga, which differed from the Christian myth in drawing its inspiration from Nature. 'The myths of these peoples led like those of ancient Greece from a contemplation of Nature to the shaping of gods and heroes. One of them – the Siegfried saga – can be traced with considerable clarity back to its seed, which can teach us not a little about the character of myth generally. Here we see natural phenomena such as day and night, the rising and the setting of the sun, condensed by imagination into personalities, to be honoured or feared according to their deeds. These personalities were then eventually changed from man-made gods into human heroes who were imagined once to have really existed, and from whom living generations and tribes proudly claimed to have sprung.' This mythology grew in time to become a religion based on Nature, and thus it might have remained if Christianity had not entered the northern countries and destroyed their religion at its roots.

'If it never succeeded in uprooting the old religion entirely, it did at any rate deprive it of its vigorously creative artistic power,' Wagner concluded. The events related in the Nordic sagas lived on, but they became scattered and distorted and lost their power over the inward thoughts and feelings. Arthurian legend, with its seemingly incomprehensible and arbitrary outlook, was the outcome of a fusion of pagan and Christian mythologies, and it was mixtures such as this that altered the character of myth entirely. Another contributing factor lay in the crusades of medieval times, which brought people from many lands together. 'If in myth it was the familiar that people sought, now, having lost all feeling for the familiar, they sought a substitute in constant newness and strangeness.'

Wagner's contention was that mythology's loss of impact was the first step towards the creation of 'political man', whose outlook is preconditioned by the demands of society organised for convenience into a state. Christianity was unable to bridge the gap between the law-abiding state and the primal urges of the individual human being, since essentially it owed its own existence to the very presence of that gap. 'If the individual were completely reconciled to society, if he found within it full satisfaction of his longing for bliss, the need for a Christian outlook would be entirely removed, and Christianity itself would for all practical purposes be destroyed.' In order to maintain its existence in a political world, the church assumed political power itself and thus became as much an enemy to the free human spirit as the state already was. With the onset of recorded history the assault on instinctive individual feeling became even more widespread: mankind's desire to discover and understand the reality behind his existence led to ever longer voyages of exploration and ever wider scientific researches, and with the huge increase in knowledge there came a new error: faced with this mass of unrelated detail, historians were tempted, in an effort to find some sort of sense in it, to make connections that could be as fanciful as those of the myth-makers and as arbitrary as those of the medieval romance writers.

This is the condition that Wagner described as political – one in which the human form is 'wrapped in the costume of history or the uniform of the state' – and the conclusion he drew from it was that the world's tragedy lay in the constant clash between the urge of the individual to follow his natural instincts and the desire of the community to establish some control over these in the cause of general well-being, and in mankind's failure to comprehend their true connection with each other. Natural instinct, he wrote, shows itself at its strongest in the physical urges of an individual, though it can also be discerned, in an arbitrary and less comprehensible form, in the moral outlook of a community. The individual's life instinct always finds new and direct expression, whereas the outlook of a community is based on habit and is therefore a conditional one. 'The outlook of the community, so long as it is not yet able to understand the intrinsic nature of individuality and its own origin from within it, is consequently a restrictive, frustrating one, and, the more vitalising and innovative individuality follows its unconscious urge to fight against habit, the more tyrannical that community will become.' The Greeks, Wagner maintained, misunderstood this urge, attributing it to some cause over which the troublesome individual himself had no control. They saw his unlawful deed as the result of a curse under which he was suffering. 'This curse, which in mythology is presented as divine punishment down to the last generation for some ancient sin, is in fact nothing but a symbol of the power of instinct that lies in the unconscious natural behaviour of the individual being, against the background of which the community seems conscious, arbitrary and in truth in need of explanation and exoneration. But it can be explained and exonerated only if one is prepared to acknowledge that the community's outlook is also instinctive and its awareness based on a mistaken interpretation of individuality.'

Frequently, when Wagner felt caught up in the mesh of theoretical argument, he turned to metaphor to disentangle himself, and here he chose to subject a familiar classical tale, the Theban legend, to a detailed scrutiny in order to illustrate more clearly the difference between individual and community instincts. This difference, and the conflicts that arise out of it, form the basic theme of Wagner's own Siegfried dramas, and thus this close analysis of the Oedipus legend is worth reproducing in full for the light it throws on Wagner's wide-ranging creative methods.

'Oedipus,' he wrote, 'had killed a man who provoked him and finally forced him into an act of self-defence. Public opinion found nothing reprehensible in this, for such occurrences were frequent, and the necessity of warding off an attack was clearly understood by all. Even less guilty of a crime was Oedipus in marrying, as a reward for a beneficent act towards the country, its widowed queen.

'However, it was then discovered that the murdered man had been not only the husband of this queen but also Oedipus's father – and thus the widow was his own mother.

'A child's love and respect for his father, and the loving

determination to look after and protect him in his old age were such involuntary feelings, and the community's outlook was so instinctively based on these feelings, that a deed which so mortally transgressed them must appear to all its members both incomprehensible and damnable. So strong were these feelings and so compelling, that even the knowledge that the father had been the first to seek the life of his own son was not enough to stifle them. Certainly Laius's death was seen to have been a deserved punishment for his earlier crime, and so we feel no particular sympathy for him, but this consideration is nevertheless insufficient to reconcile us to Oedipus's deed, which, however one looks at it, had been, and still was patricide.

'Public revulsion against Oedipus was greater, however, for having married his own mother and fathered children by her. In family life, the most natural, but also the most intensive form of community, the affection between parents and children and between the children themselves takes an entirely different form from the sudden and violent eruption of sexual love. Within the family the natural bonds between begetters and begotten become the bonds of habit, and it is from habit too that natural affection arises between brothers and sisters. The first stirrings of sexual love come to young people from outside, and the urge is so overwhelming that it draws them away from the accustomed family surroundings, in which the urge had never been felt, to face the unaccustomed. Sexual love is the stimulant that breaks through the narrow confines of the family in order to widen it into a still larger social unit. The concept of family love as opposed to sexual love is therefore an instinctive one, deduced from the perceived nature of things: it is based on experience and habit, and in consequence it is a strong concept, stirring our emotions irresistibly.

'Oedipus, who married his mother and fathered children by her, is a figure who fills us with horror and disgust, for his actions unforgivably offend against our *habit-formed* relationship with our own mother and our views as shaped by that relationship.

'Are these views, now grown into moral concepts, so strong just because they arise involuntarily from our feelings concerning human nature? If that is the case, we must now ask whether Oedipus sinned against human nature when he married his mother. Most certainly he did not. If he had sinned in that way, Nature would surely have expressed its displeasure by allowing no children to spring from the marriage. But Nature proved quite amenable: Jocasta and Oedipus, who met as two people unknown to each other, fell in love, and their love was shattered only when they learned from outside that they were mother and son. Oedipus and Jocasta had not known in what relationship they stood from a social point of view: they had acted unconsciously in accordance with the natural instincts of individual human beings. Their union resulted in an enrichment of human society through two sturdy sons and two noble daughters, on whose heads, as on those of their parents, society's remorseless curse now lay. Their parents, aware of their position within this moral society, passed sentence on themselves once they learned of their unwitting sin against morality. By destroying themselves as an act of atonement, they demonstrated the strength of social revulsion against their marriage, a revulsion that, before their marriage, they had shared through force of habit. That they had nevertheless perpetrated the deed, despite their social conscience, was proof of the far greater and less resistible power of the individual's unconscious human nature.

'How very significant it becomes in the light of this that Oedipus should have been the one person to solve the sphinx's riddle [What goes on four feet in the morning, on two feet at noon, and on three feet in the evening?]! When Oedipus named the *human being* as the answer to the riddle, he spoke in advance his justification and at the same time his condemnation. It was above all the human individual in thrall to Nature that he recognised in the half-bestial body of the sphinx, and after the part-human beast had flung itself from its lonely rock and dashed itself to pieces in the chasm below, this clever solver of riddles turned to the cities of man so that the complete human being, the social human being, might be guessed from his own downfall. As he plucked out those shining eyes that had burned with anger against an insolent despot and shone with love for a noble woman without realising that the former was his father and the latter his mother, he was flinging himself down to join the shattered sphinx, whose riddle he had then to acknowledge as still unsolved. Now we ourselves have to solve this riddle, and to accomplish it by finding room for individual instinct within society itself, of which it is the highest adornment, ever renewing and imparting new life.

'But let us first follow the Oedipus legend further to see how *society* behaved, and the false paths along which its moral conscience led it.

'Creon, Jocasta's brother, came to power in Thebes owing to quarrels between Oedipus's sons. He gave orders that the body of Polynices, who had been slain in a duel with his brother Eteocles, should be left unburied, exposed to wind and birds, whereas that of Eteocles, who had also died in the duel, should be buried with full honours: anyone acting against this command would be buried alive. Antigone, the brothers' sister – she who had accompanied her blind father into exile – defied the command in full consciousness, buried the corpse of her disgraced brother and suffered the prescribed punishment.

'Here we see the state that had imperceptibly emerged out of this community absorbing sustenance from the habits formed by its general outlook: it had now become their agent, in that it represented the abstraction of habits born of fear and dislike of the unaccustomed. Armed with the power of custom, the state now turned destructively against the community itself by denying it for its existence the natural nourishment it had gained from its most instinctive and most sacred social feelings. The Oedipus myth shows us exactly how this came about, so let us examine it more closely.

'What was Creon hoping to gain from his cruel command? And what allowed him to assume that such a command would *not* be indignantly rejected by the people? After their father's downfall, Eteocles and Polynices had decided to share their heritage, the rule over Thebes, by taking turns in occupying the throne. Eteocles held it first, but when Polynices returned from voluntary exile at the appointed time to take power for his agreed period, Eteocles refused to hand it over. He thus broke his oath. Did the community, that believed in the sanctity of oaths, punish him for this breach? No, it supported him in his behaviour. Did that mean that respect for the sanctity of oaths had already been lost? No, on the contrary: the people complained to the gods of the evils of oath-breaking, for they feared it would be avenged. Yet, despite their guilty conscience, the citizens of Thebes approved Eteocles's action, since the *content* of the oath, the brothers' sworn agreement, seemed to them at that moment far more irksome than the consequences of its having been broken, consequences that could perhaps be averted by sacrifices and offerings to the gods. What they did not like was a change of ruler, everlasting renewal:

15

habit had already established itself as the true lawgiver. The citizens' siding with Eteocles was also evidence of a practical instinct in regard to property, which everyone wishes to enjoy on his own, not to share with another: every citizen who regarded property as a guarantee of accustomed peace shared in fact the guilt for the unbrotherly act of the chief property owner, Eteocles. So Eteocles was supported by the power of self-interested habit, and it was against this that the betrayed brother Polynices fought with such youthful ardour. All he was conscious of inside himself was a wound that cried out for vengeance. He gathered together an army of heroic companions who felt as he did, marched on the oath-breaking city and pressed hard for the expulsion of the brother who was robbing him of his inheritance. To the Thebans this thoroughly justified action seemed a monstrous crime, for Polynices, by warring against his native city, was undeniably showing himself to be a very poor patriot. Polynices's friends had come together from many different lands, drawn by a purely human interest in his cause, and thus they represented society in its widest and most natural aspect, a purely human society confronting a limited, narrow-minded, self-seeking community that even before their forceful intervention was imperceptibly becoming petrified into a state. To end the long war the brothers challenged each other to single combat, and it left them both dead on the battlefield.

'Wise Creon now reviewed the situation and saw the drift of public opinion, at the centre of which he detected habit, anxiety and dislike of novelty. The view of society as a moral force, which in great-hearted Oedipus had been so strong that he destroyed himself in horror over his unconscious crime, was forced to give way when its purely human element came into conflict with what was society's strongest concern, with established custom, that is to say, with common self-interest.

At all points where it conflicted with the common practices of society, this moral conscience stepped aside and established itself as *religion*, while practical society formed itself into a *state*. Morality, which previously had been something warm and living within the community, became in the framework of religion something merely cerebral, desirable but no longer attainable. The state's criterion, on the other hand, was practical usefulness, and, if in the pursuit of it the moral conscience was injured, matters could soon be put right by religious ceremonies that did no harm to the state. In this arrangement the great advantage, for the church as well as for the state, was that someone was gained on whom the blame for one's sins could be laid: for state crimes the monarch could shoulder the consequences, while for offences against religious morality the gods had to answer. Eteocles was for all practical purposes the new state's scapegoat: the kind gods had only to visit the consequences of his oath-breaking on Eteocles himself, while the doughty citizens of Thebes could be left to enjoy the stability of the state for themselves (or so they hoped, though unfortunately for them it never came to pass!). Some new person who would now be willing to take on the role of scapegoat was therefore very welcome to them. That person was wise Creon, a man who surely knew how to keep on the right side of the gods, and not, thank goodness, hot-headed Polynices, who had banged so wildly on the doors of the worthy city just because of a simple case of oath-breaking.

'Aware as he was of the true cause of the Laïds' tragic downfall, Creon had realised how indulgent the Thebans could be towards genuine crimes, as long as these did not disturb the peaceful routine of citizen existence. The Pythia had told Laius that he would one day be killed by a son yet to be born to him. It was only to avoid causing a public nuisance that the worthy father gave secret orders for his newborn son to be killed in some remote corner of the forest, thus providing proof of his remarkable consideration for the tender consciences of the Theban citizens. If the murder had been committed openly in front of their eyes, they would have been vexed, both by the scandal and the obligation it imposed on them to pray much longer than usual to the gods. On no account, however, would they have felt the horror that would have led them to prevent the deed being committed and to punish the intending murderer of his son. Their horror would at once have been stifled by the realisation that this murder would guarantee them the peace and quiet that a son would be bound to disturb – at any rate, a son who some time in the future would behave undutifully. Creon had observed that the revelation of Laius's inhuman deed had aroused no great anger against the deed itself. It had in fact even looked as if the citizens would have been happier if the murder had been done, for in that case everything would have been as it should be and the terrible scandal in Thebes that plunged its citizens into so many years of unrest would never have arisen. *Peace and quiet*, even at the price of the most despicable crime possible against human nature and indeed against established morality, the deliberate killing of one's own child for self-seeking motives of a most unfatherly kind – peace and quiet were surely more worth preserving than those most natural of human feelings that tell a father he should sacrifice himself to his children, not the other way around. So what had this community, whose foundations had once rested on natural moral feelings, now become? It had become the direct opposite of what it had once stood for, a symbol for immorality and hypocrisy. And the poison that had caused its ruin was – *habit*. The propensity for habit, for undisturbed peace, had lured it into blocking up the source that could have kept it eternally fresh and healthy. This source was the free individual, acting according to his own nature. Only through an individual could morality, that is to say, the truly human element, be restored to a community in its final stage of degradation, an individual acting according to the instinctive urge of natural feeling and morally defying the community. This noble vindication of true human nature is also given prominence in the universal myth with which we are dealing.

'Creon was now ruler. In him the people saw the legitimate successor to Laius and Eteocles, and he confirmed his legitimacy in the eyes of the citizens when he sentenced the body of the unpatriotic Polynices to the appalling shame of being left unburied, his soul thereby condemned to eternal unrest. It was a decision of very great political wisdom. Through it Creon consolidated his own power by exonerating Eteocles, who had ensured the citizens' peace by breaking his oath, and in that way he gave them a clear assurance that he too was prepared to preserve the state's peace and quiet by taking on himself all sins against true human morality. Additionally, by his order he gave the clearest and strongest proof of his own state-loving outlook: giving humanity a slap in the face, he cried – Long live the state!

'Within the walls of this state there beat just one lonely, mourning heart in which humanity had found refuge. It was the heart of a sweet virgin in whose depths the flower of *love* blossomed in awesome beauty. Antigone knew nothing of politics: she *loved*. Did she seek to defend Polynices? Did she set out to search for considerations, connections, points of law that might explain, excuse or justify his conduct? No, she simply loved him. Did she love him because he was her brother? Was not Eteocles her brother too, and Oedipus and Jocasta their parents? After all those terrible experiences could she think of her family bonds other than with horror?

Could she have been expected to learn the power of love from natural bonds so cruelly torn apart? No, she loved Polynices because he was unhappy, and only the utmost power of love could free him from the curse that lay on his head. So what was this love that was not sexual love, not the love of parents and children, not the love of brothers and sisters? It was the finest blossom of all. From the ruins of sexual love and family love that society had disowned and the state denied the richest flower grew, nourished by the seeds of all those types of love – the flower of pure *charity*.

'Antigone's love was fully conscious. She knew what she was doing – but she also knew that she must do it, that she had no other choice and had to act according to the dictates of love. She knew that she had to obey this compelling, though unconscious need to destroy herself out of sympathy, and in this consciousness of the unconscious within her she was completely human, representing love at its highest and most powerful. Antigone was saying to the pious citizens of Thebes: You condemned my father and my mother because unknowingly they loved each other; but you did not condemn Laius, the knowing murderer of his son, and you protected Eteocles, the enemy of his brother. Now condemn me for acting out of pure charity – then your cup of iniquity will be full. And what happened? *Antigone's love curse destroyed the state!*

'Not a hand was raised in her favour as she was led to her death. The citizens wept and prayed to the gods to relieve them of the pain sympathy for the unhappy woman was causing them; they walked beside her and comforted her with the assurance that there was no other way: the state's peace and quiet unfortunately required them to sacrifice their humanity.

'But in the place where all love is born, love's avenger was also born. A youth ardently loved Antigone: he revealed his feelings to his father and appealed to his paternal love to show mercy for the condemned woman. Harshly repulsed, the youth stormed the grave in which she had been buried alive. He found her already dead, and with his own sword pierced his loving heart. This youth was the son of Creon, the state in person. Seeing the body of the son who had been forced by love to curse his father, the ruler became a father again. His son's sword of love cut remorsefully into his heart: the state, wounded to its uttermost depths, crumbled to dust and in death became human.

'Blessed Antigone, on thee I now call! Raise high thy banner, that beneath it we may destroy and redeem!'

After this passionate and psychologically penetrating re-telling of the Oedipus myth – one which, in Wagner's own words, provides 'a clear picture of the whole history of man-kind from the beginnings of society to the necessary downfall of the state' – it is disconcerting to learn from Cosima Wagner's diaries that he came in later years to consider his views on the state versus the individual to have been 'immature and erroneous as a concept'. However, they were of vast importance in helping him to find a dramatic form for his own attempt at tackling in *Der Ring des Nibelungen* the moral problems he discerned in the Oedipus legend.

More will be said about that in the next chapter. Let us now return to the more general implications of the argument that Wagner was striving to illustrate with his analysis.

It was, he felt, only through an acceptance of human nature, and recognition of the unconscious and instinctive elements within it, that a way could be found through the artificialities of modern civilisation based on habit and preconceived ideas to the true feelings of the individual human being. The main practical difficulty in achieving this was that communication in our modern era is channelled through the intellect, which has itself been conditioned by the state. 'From our first youthful impression onwards we see a human being only in the form and character the state has given him. To our unconscious feeling the individuality in which the state has dressed him appears as his true nature, and we can grasp him only through those distinctive qualities that are in truth not his own, but lent him by the state.'

The aim of drama must therefore be a return from intellect to feeling, and that would be achieved by replacing *supposed* by real individuality. Drama is the most consummate of the arts, Wagner declared, since it utilises all the expressive capabilities of a human being, and because of this the dramatist is in the best position to reach the emotions of his audience, for his approach is through all the senses, the most direct route to feeling. 'Drama differs from all the other literary arts in its ability fully to conceal its aim through the complete reality of its presentation . . . The dramatist's skill lies in merging his aim so completely in the fabric that *understanding becomes emotion*. Only in this way will he achieve his aim, which is to bring before our eyes and senses the things of life in all their spontaneity, thus justifying life through its own necessities, for it is these alone, life's necessities, that feelings can understand.'

During the performance of a dramatic work nothing must be left for the analysing intellect to seek. 'In drama we must become aware through our emotions. Our intellect will tell us, "Thus it is," only after our emotions have told us, "Thus it must be." Emotions, however, can be felt only in their own particular way: they know no language other than their own. Things that can be explained to us only through the all-accommodating intellect leave the emotions uncomprehending and dissatisfied.' The dramatist's task, therefore, is not to invent dramatic actions, but to take a subject arising out of emotional needs and make it so understandable that we have no need at all to call on our intellect to justify it.

The choice calls for care. Historical subjects with no immediate relevance to the period in which we live can appeal only to our intellect, not our emotions, and, since the intellect demands reasons, the dramatist is forced at some stage to reveal his reason for his choice by plainly pointing the moral. 'Action that seeks justification from and through the emotions is not concerned with a moral. What moral there is lies solely in the vindication of the action by instinctive human feelings.' Consequently it can only be of the kind with which human feelings are most concerned and which is of permanent interest, unaffected by historical or political considerations.

However, no action in life exists in isolation: each individual act is connected in some way to the acts of others, and the greater the strength of feeling actuating the central figure in the chosen action, the more emphatically and comprehensively must it be shown in relation to others. It is the dramatist's task to select from the many possible protagonists only those who contribute to a full understanding of the action and help concentrate attention on the central figure or figures.

The need to concentrate a dramatic action in order to make it immediately accessible to the emotions led Wagner to consider the use of what he termed '*Wunder*' (miracle, marvel), taking care to explain that he was not using the word in the religious sense of a mysterious act defying rational explanation, but rather in the sense of what we in English might call 'magic'. His argument, baldly stated, was that it is through the imagination that intellect communicates with feeling, and the dramatist, who of necessity must make use of his own intellect in shaping his drama, can take advantage, for reasons of dramatic economy, of the ability of instinctive feeling to accept without question a symbolic rather than a realistic approach to certain actions. In his desire to make his chosen action understandable, the dramatist is in any case obliged to concentrate events in a way that distinguishes them from real life. 'The human being, distracted by the interventions of time and space, may very well fail to understand his own life activities. The dramatist places before him a picture of these activities, condensed for ease of understanding, with everything concentrated into one single tense situation. This situation may indeed seem unusual and fantastic in isolation, but, its novelty and fantasy being self-contained, it is not seen by the audience as "magic", but accepted as an understandable depiction of reality.'

Magic of this kind enables the dramatist to bring even the most disparate elements together into a connected whole while remaining in touch with Nature, since what he is showing us, even in his most unusual figurations, is not a perversion of Nature, but a poetic use of natural phenomena to provide an image that an artistic human being can grasp.

In his treatment of *Wunder* Wagner was clearly arguing from the standpoint of a long-held conviction, for this particular 'magic' ingredient had been a part of all his dramatic works from *Der Fliegende Holländer* onwards: one has only to think of the phantom ship in that work, of the Venusberg in *Tannhäuser* and the swan in *Lohengrin*, and the symbolic use of magic in that sense is a commonplace of myths. Essentially, all he had now done was to confirm through reasoning what his instinct had already told him: that the ideal drama would seek its subject matter in myth and not in history. 'The incomparable thing about myth,' he wrote, 'is that it is always true, and its content, however densely packed, inexhaustible for all ages.' And, having established that, he summed up the implications in practical terms: 'All we now have to ask ourselves is by what expressive means this myth can be most intelligibly conveyed in dramatic terms, and to do this we must return to that factor in the work that determines its whole nature. This is the necessary *justification for the dramatic action through its motivations*, and to achieve this the creative intelligence addresses instinctive *feeling* in order to win understanding for the action through its spontaneous sympathy. We have seen that the condensation – for practical reasons of intelligibility – of the many elements comprising the action, widely scattered as they would be in reality, was due to the dramatist's desire to present a large variety of connected factors in human life in the only way that enables one to grasp their necessity. To achieve this condensation it was necessary for him to include in the situations chosen for representation not only motivations immediately relevant to them, but also motivations for things not shown on stage, and to justify these to the emotions by presenting them as a strengthening of the principal motivations . . . Finally we saw that this strengthening of the dramatic situation could be achieved only by raising that situation above the common human level through the use of magical elements which, while remaining within the limits of credibility, increased human faculties and sensibilities to a point unattainable in normal life.'

By a 'strengthening' of the motivations, Wagner went on to explain, he meant the absorption of all subsidiary interests in a single overriding one that so takes possession of the central figure of the drama that his emotional responses are in an either positive or negative way entirely dominated by it.

In preparing for the vital moment at which the actual

drama begins, the dramatist makes use of word language, which, since the aim at this stage is to define and compare, is the only appropriate one for making his meaning clear. Once this has been done, and the way opened for emotional expression, word language is no longer adequate, unless the dramatist can intensify it in the way he has already intensified the motivations, and this he can do only through merging word language into sound language.

'Sound language is the beginning and end of word language, just as *feeling* is the beginning and end of intellect, *myth* the beginning and end of history, and *lyricism* the beginning and end of poetry. The mediating factor between beginning and centre point, as also between this and the point of departure, is the *imagination*.'

With this cryptic statement Wagner set off at last on his quest for the right balance between words and music in drama and the best means of relating each to the other. His first concern was with the basic nature of words and the origins of language, and he showed at once his allegiance to the school that believes in vowel sounds as the primitive expression of pleasure, grief, anger or pain. The degree of intensity in the feeling, he suggested, was shown through a vehemence that led to variations in the pitch of the vowel sound and by accompanying bodily gestures that introduced the concept of rhythm. He termed the result 'rhythmic melody' and concluded that verse metres developed from this combination of sound and movement rather than the other way round. Consonants came into use as a means of identifying the objects to which feeling was referring, and these 'clothed' sounds, as Wagner called them, formed the roots of all articulate language as it eventually evolved. In its early stages language was still just an expression of feeling, and alliteration, which he named as the first step towards arranging words in a formal pattern, served the purpose of identifying relationships between objects through similarities of sound, at the same time adding emphasis by thus linking them together.

'As long as human beings kept Nature in view and were able to feel at one with it, thus long were they able to invent word roots to characterise objects and their relevance to each other. When, under the growing pressures of life, they turned their backs on this rich source of their linguistic powers, their inventive powers shrivelled as well.' The direct connection that existed between words and feeling was progressively lost, word roots were forgotten, and that 'mother melody' of alliteration that arose from the desire for emphasis was reduced to an end rhyme 'fluttering loosely at the end of melodic phrases'. The final stage of this development was prose, the vocabulary of which was based on convention: it could not express feelings, only describe them. In this, the everyday language we learned at school, 'we cannot really convey an innermost feeling, since in this language we cannot *invent* in line with that feeling. All we can do is transmit our feelings to the intellect, but not to the emotions which could be relied on to understand them; and it is therefore quite logical that at this stage of our modern evolution we should seek refuge from purely intellectual language in pure sound language, in our present-day music.'

At this point Wagner closed the second part of *Opera and Drama*. In the third part, which in his letter to Uhlig in December 1850 he described as the most important, he dealt directly with the practical collaboration of composer and librettist – a word that he would have scorned in relation to a work of his, preferring to call the writer of the text a poet. 'The difference in character between a poet and a composer,' he wrote, 'is that the poet has compressed a widely scattered number of actions, emotions and expressive moments, discernible only through the intellect, to a point at which feeling is engaged to the greatest possible extent. The composer has now to expand this densely packed point to the full range of its emotional content.'

The poet's part in the collaboration does not end in merely providing the emotionally charged dramatic framework: he must also find the words that will enable the composer effectively to carry out his task of expansion, and this entails an examination of the origin and function of verbal rhythms – or, in other words, metre. The rhythm of ancient Greek verse had been dictated by the dance movements to which it was spoken, but, since no evidence of the bodily movements and the music to which they were made have come down to us, their validity as a model is much reduced, especially as the languages of modern times tend to place stresses at different points. The natural rhythm of these languages – and here Wagner was obviously thinking only of the Germanic languages – is that 'five-footed monster we call iambics', a metre he considered not only ugly, but 'in itself offensive to feeling', since 'its clattering trot must in the end rob the listener of all sense and understanding.'

In both these metres, the classical and the iambic, rhythm gave form to the melody, whose function was therefore a subsidiary one. End rhyme was the outcome of what Wagner called 'Christian melody', best recognised in early church chorales. These possessed no marked rhythm: they moved along evenly, note by note, until the breath gave out: 'In them language had no justification beyond its ability to dissolve into an expression of feeling whose content was fear of the Lord and a longing for death.' The end rhyme, then, was in its origin merely a device to cover up a physical limitation, but it was then taken over by Latin nations – whose verse has no accents but only a fixed number of syllables – as a way of identifying their words as poetry and not prose. Wagner had little respect for end rhyme. If, he maintained, the purpose of poetry is acknowledged to be an appeal to feeling through a heightened means of expression, rhyme runs the risk of missing its aim by drawing attention away from the sense into mere pleasure in the repeated sound.

All kinds of verbal accentuation, whether metrical systems or end rhymes, evolved at a time when music was still a primitive art. As it developed and created rules of its own, a new complication arose: musical patterns seldom, if ever, corresponded exactly with existing verse patterns. A composer who attempted to mould his melody exactly to the formal requirements of the verse would rob his melody of the chance to reveal its own sensuous beauty, thus also rendering it powerless to raise the verse to a gripping expression of feeling. The composer normally found it more practical to write his melody as a self-contained entity that might indeed reflect the sentiments expressed in the poem, but only in a very general way. The consequence of this approach was that in modern vocal music words came to occupy a position 'no bigger than that of the caption to a painting.'

It was certainly not a relationship with which Wagner could remain content, for he held the view that only through words could the emotions that music can arouse become fully articulate. His search for the perfect marriage between music and words having produced, in his examination of existing forms, no solution that could satisfy him, he felt himself forced to return to the beginnings and to work out a new form of his own, and it turned out to be one based on practical as well as theoretical considerations. 'A faithful observance of the expressions we use when our feelings are aroused, even in everyday life, should provide the poet with a reliable measure of the number of accents in a spontaneous phrase. In moments of real emotion, when we throw all conventionally extended modern phrases to the winds, we always try to express ourselves shortly and sharply and as decisively as possible *within a single breath*; and in this loaded utterance we accentuate, through the force of our emotion, far more strongly than usual, at times placing the stresses close together and dwelling on them with raised voice. In this way we impress their importance on the feelings of others as well as on our own. The number of accents involuntarily forming a phrase or the main part of a phrase within a single breath will vary according to the nature of the roused feeling: an angry, active emotion will use a fairly large number of stresses, whereas deep suffering will certainly spread the breath over fewer, but more drawn-out accents.'

Rising and falling accents, in sentences shorn of all words not vitally necessary to express the required emotion, form the natural basis of rhythm in spoken verse, and through musical rhythm they can be both precisely defined and infinitely varied. Such accents will inevitably fall on words, or parts of words, of purely human content to which feeling is most responsive; 'thus they will invariably fall on word roots which applied originally, not just to a particular object, but also to the feeling this object aroused in us.'

Wagner's 'return to the roots' – in this case to the roots of words which were the first conscious attempts of human beings to express their feelings – may owe more to intuition than to science, but for him it had the strength of conviction. As already mentioned, by root he meant the original open vowel sound that, according to his belief, defined the nature of the emotion in general, together with its associated consonants that defined the particular cause of the emotion. The function of consonants was to give precise meaning to a single word, and the emotional responses aroused in the listener by this word could be heightened by use, within the phrase containing it, of other words with a similar consonantal sound. These would engage the attention and stir the emotions by reason of the implied kinship.

This is a very general summary of an argument that Wagner developed over several pages to prove that alliteration, or *Stabreim*, to give it its more concrete German name, offered the most rewarding prospect for his own works. It was no new discovery, for the text of *Siegfrieds Tod*, which was already in existence, was fully alliterative. Incidentally, it is interesting to note in this connection that Wagner's efforts in *Opera and Drama* to pin down his intuitions by intense examination did not lead him, as they might have done, into setting up a dogma to be unswervingly followed, but rather the opposite. The extravagant alliteration of *Siegfrieds Tod* was considerably toned down when he revised that work and renamed it *Götterdämmerung*. Lines such as '*Nie ritt ein Recke edleres Ross*' were jettisoned entirely – but not his firm belief in the value of consonants, which he continued to emphasise throughout his life: we shall meet them again in the chapter on actor-singers.

Having now analysed the function of words in drama down from the general to the minutest particular in the shape of vowel sounds and consonant sounds, Wagner had reached the point at which their union with music could be considered in its most elemental form, and from here onwards he proceeded in the opposite direction: from the particular to the general. Contemplating the text as finished and the poet's work as already done, he observed: 'It was only through the consonants of alliterative word roots that the poet had been able to disclose to the emotions, and through them to the understanding, associations between the words he had chosen to accent.' The composer, taking over from him, had not just one connecting device at his disposal, but an infinite number in the shape of musical notes that could be used in various combinations and series to cover the whole phrase, thus conveying to feeling associations between all its parts, not just the accented ones.

By thus pointing out the superior resources of music over words in affecting the emotions, Wagner left one in no doubt which he considered to be the dominant factor, and he went on to state quite categorically that from the moment a word is sung, not spoken, music takes over as the main conveyor of feeling to the senses, 'and musical feeling alone now governs the choice and the significance of both the leading and the subsidiary notes.' All the same, he was not prepared to dismiss the significance of words on that account, and in his search for the point of balance he made use of a metaphor. Defining melody as a horizontal deployment of the notes forming a harmonic chord, he likened it to a mirror reflection on the surface of the sea of the poet's creation, to which the composer rises 'from the harmonic depths to the surface on which the rapturous marriage between the begetting poetic thought and music's infinite birth-giving powers will be celebrated.'

The sea metaphor was retained when, some pages later, Wagner applied his thoughts about words and music to the Ninth Symphony of Beethoven. 'From the ground note of harmony,' he wrote, 'music had spread to a huge and varied expanse in which the composer of absolute music, swimming without rest or purpose, at last began to feel fear: before him he saw nothing but an endless surge of possibilities . . . and he yearned for the quiet bays of his homeland, where the water flowed peacefully on familiar currents.'

These quiet bays were the simple melodies recognisable in

genuine folksong, 'that motherly primal melody from which the language of words was once born', but which had been forgotten as poetry grew more and more intellectual. It was Beethoven, 'the boldest of swimmers', who led the way back when he felt the urge for words that would define more clearly the feelings he was striving to express in his Ninth Symphony. The 'patriarchal' melody, as Wagner called Beethoven's setting of the opening words of Schiller's 'Ode to Joy', did not emerge *out of* that poem, but rather – having been invented away from the written verse – was just spread over it. This melody 'can be seen as wholly restricted to those tonal relationships familiar in the old kind of national folksong. It contains next to no modulation, and its simplicity in terms of key shows quite clearly that it was a deliberate return on the composer's part to the historical source of music. This was a necessary step in the context of absolute music not based on poetry: a composer wishing to speak clearly to the emotions through music alone can do so only by scaling down his infinite resources to a very restricted level. Beethoven, when he wrote that melody down, was saying: "This is the only way in which we absolute musicians can make our message fully understood." But in human affairs the path to development lies not in a return to the old, but in progress: return is artificial, never natural. Beethoven's return to patriarchal melody was – like the melody itself – artificial. His artistic purpose did not lie in the mere construction of this melody: we see rather how deliberately he scaled down his powers of melodic invention for an instant in order to stand on the natural ground from which music sprang, a ground on which he could hold out his hand to the poet and take the poet's hand in his. When, with this simple, limited melody, he felt the poet's hand in his own, he moved ahead with the poem, shaping it in line with its inner spirit and its form into a tonal structure of ever-increasing boldness and intricacy, in order to bring forth wonders from the storehouse of poetic musical language such as we had never heard before, wonders such as "*Seid umschlungen, Millionen!*", "*Ahnest du den Schöpfer, Welt?*" and the utterly convincing bringing together of "*Seid umschlungen*" with "*Freude, schöner Götterfunken!*" If we now compare the broad melodic structure of the musical setting of the complete "*Seid umschlungen*" stanza with the melody the great composer took from his store of absolute music and, so to speak, spread out over the "*Freude, schöner Götterfunken*" stanza, we shall gain a precise understanding of the distinction between what I called "patriarchal melody" and melody that grows out of the words expressing the poetic purpose.'

This second, and more complicated form of melody uses modulation to arouse and to intensify feeling, and this led Wagner to reflect on the relationship between key and melody. The movement out of the original key, he wrote, arises from the poetic aim as presented in the text. 'The main notes of the melody are in a sense the young and growing members of the family who are striving for independence outside their familiar surroundings. They win independence, however, not as egoists, but through contact with another person from outside the family. The virgin achieves independence from her own family only through the love of a young man who, as scion of a different family, draws the virgin over to his side. Thus the note that steps outside its own key is one that has already been attracted and determined by another key, and it is into this key it must now merge in accordance with the dictates of love.'

An interesting aspect here is the nature of the metaphor that Wagner chose to make his point. Throughout *Opera and Drama* his insistence on 'feeling' is constantly recurring, and his overall metaphor, in which drama is seen as a sexual union between poetry as the man and music as the woman, is subdivided into many others, such as the one we have just met, connected with love. The purpose is clear: it is to keep firmly before our eyes (and before his own as well) that even in such dry subjects as the technicalities of composition the emotions must not be forgotten. And the technical aspect he next considered – the use of modulation – still echoes that theme: 'The leading note that effects the change from one key to another,' he wrote, 'can be interpreted only as impelled by love.'

What part do words play in calling for modulation? If the poet's alliterative line of verse refers only to a single emotion, Wagner decided, there would be no incentive to move outside the chosen key, whereas, when the words reflect conflicting emotions, the composer would recognise the need for a change of key. Here, in the balance between words and music, the dominant position seems to have reverted to the poet, but Wagner found a compensatory factor for the composer: the poet may decide the mood, but it is the composer who, with his more fluid resources, gives it depth and conveys it in all its subtlety.

Before passing on to the next technical point, the role of harmony in modulation, Wagner inserted a passage on the significance of keys that deserves to be quoted in full (though at times more paraphrased than translated) for the bearing it has on a work that, as far as we know, was not yet present even in his unconscious thoughts – a work, however, that would illustrate far more vividly than any amount of theorising the point he was striving to make concerning the deployment of keys. That work is *Tristan und Isolde*.

Two of the poetic lines Wagner chose as expressive of contrasting emotions were 'Love brings joy and sorrow' and 'But in its woe is woven bliss', both of which are alliterative in German ('*Die Liebe bringt Lust und Leid*' and '*Doch in ihr Weh auch webt sie Wonnen*'). He now asked us to assume that between these two lines there lay a lengthy series of lines dealing with the feelings aroused along the way from one to the other before a final return to the principal feeling: 'In order to realise the poetic aim, musical modulation would have to pass through many different keys and back again. Each of these keys would, however, appear in a clear relationship to the original key, and that key would determine the particular light the new key throws on the expression and also to a certain extent, by its very presence, it would enable this light to be shed. As ground note of each particular sentiment aroused, the principal key would reveal its association with all keys and thus, as a sentiment is being expressed, make its own presence felt so intensely and so extensively that only matters associated with that sentiment could control our emotions during the time it is being expressed. Our emotional capacity in general, because of the exalted broadness of the exposition, would be fully absorbed by this sentiment, which would then become an all-embracing one, unerringly intelligible to every human being.

'A poetical-musical passage thus controlled by a principal key might be called a "period", and for the time being we might maintain that the most expressive work of art will be that in which many such periods are displayed to the full, each helping to shape the next and, in pursuit of their high poetic aim, developing into a broad depiction of one aspect of human nature that can be seen as fully representative of all human nature (in the same way that a principal musical key can be seen as representative of all the other keys), and thus will most surely and most directly affect the emotions. Such a work of art would be drama at its highest, a work in which one essential aspect of human nature would impose itself on feeling with such force and such conviction through a series of logically connected emotional incidents that the dramatic action itself – the necessary condensation of an entire emotional content into a single whole – would emerge from this mass of associations as something instinctively desired and therefore fully comprehended.'

Having established that melody was the outward means of conveying that poetic appeal to the emotions which was the basic purpose of his drama, Wagner now turned his attention to harmony, which he described as 'the bearing element that takes the fertilising seed of the poetic aim and brings it to maturity, strictly according to the dictates of its own female constitution.' As such it has an important part to play, not only in supporting the melody, but also in shaping it. As already mentioned, Wagner defined melody as a horizontal deployment of the notes forming a harmonic chord, and it is the simultaneous sounding of this chord that gives each note of the melody its expressive significance.

'The progression of a melody from one key to another can only be established by a change of the ground note . . . The presence of this ground note, and the harmonic chord determined by it, is indispensable if feeling is to be enabled to grasp what the melody is striving to express. And "presence" means that the ground note must be heard . . . Only the simultaneous sounding of harmony and melody fully convinces the emotions of the emotional content of the melody: without it, the emotions would be left in a state of uncertainty.' The ear, Wagner contended, positively insists on the simultaneous sounding of harmony and melody in order to relieve its owner of this uncertainty and leave him to concentrate on the emotional message the melody is conveying. 'In consequence, the simultaneous sounding of harmony and not as a burden on the ear, but as the only way of easing its path to understanding.'

The importance Wagner attached to harmony, a purely musical resource, led him to deal rather too facilely with the possibility of coming into conflict with the poet, whose choice of emotionally charged accents in his verse might not fit well with the dictates of harmonic construction. 'The poet's melody,' he wrote, 'already contains the harmony, though it is, as it were, unspoken.' Unconsciously the poet would be choosing words with an expressive significance that conformed to the requirements of harmony, but for him it would be a matter of deliberate thought rather than direct emotional expression. What he was doing was shaping his lines according to an imagined melody that could be treated harmonically, and the composer, who alone was in a position to supply the harmony, created along with it a melody of his own.

It was perhaps difficult for Wagner, who from the very beginning was his own poet, to visualise a collaboration in which two separate individuals were involved. His assertion that the poet already had a melody in his mind's ear as he wrote his words reminds one very much of his letter of 30 January 1844 to the Berlin journalist Karl Gaillard, in which he declared he was 'thoroughly immersed in the musical aura' of his work before writing a line of the text. His lengthy and elaborate metaphor in *Opera and Drama* – the picture of a poet and a composer encircling the world in opposite directions, one by land and one by sea and changing over halfway through – is entertaining, but it hardly justifies his conclusion that after their long journey 'the poet has become a musician, the musician a poet: *together* they are now a complete artistic human being.' The most it proves is that if (unlike Wagner) the composer has to entrust the writing of his text to a separate poet, it would be an advantage for each to understand the other's business.

Wagner extended his travellers' metaphor to lead him to the next point in his discourse. 'The musician had instructed him [the poet] in the management of the tiller, the characteristics of the sails, and all the other strange and ingenious devices needed to ensure a safe voyage through wind and weather. At the tiller of this vessel sailing proudly over the waves, the poet, who had previously plodded laboriously, step by step, over hill and dale, becomes blissfully aware of the all-embracing power of the human being. Safe on his high deck, he sees the battering waves as the willing and loyal bearers of his destiny, the destiny of his poetic purpose. This ship is the mighty instrument of his powerful, wide-ranging will; he thinks with grateful love of the musician who invented it to withstand the perils of the sea and has now delivered it into his own hands – for this ship is the trusty ruler over the boundless floods of harmony: it is the *orchestra*.'

Before establishing the precise role the orchestra should play in his ideal drama, Wagner found it necessary to delve back into the historical origins of harmony and polyphony, which he identified as arising out of the yearning of a community to address its common god. Thus they are connected in the first place with the human voice, the most natural of musical instruments. Counterpoint, the next development, showed the first stirrings of individualism, which in its advanced stages gave birth to the solo opera singer, relegating the minor singers and the musical instruments to a mere accompaniment.

The kind of drama at which he was aiming was concerned entirely with individuals and their predicaments, and in it there would be no place for a chorus in the usual operatic sense, that is to say, a body of singers whose voices are used solely to fill the harmonic requirements of a particular melody. Each participant in the drama, however small his part, must be allotted words and music of his own, and the role of providing the necessary harmonic support entrusted solely to the orchestra.

This would not be its only task: far from it, indeed. An orchestra consists of a number of individual instruments, each producing notes with a tonal colour of its own. The sounds emerging from them Wagner likened to the vowel sounds of spoken language, without the consonantal sounds that only the human throat can supply. But since the sound each kind of instrument produces is unique, one can regard this particular sound as a 'consonant', identifying an emotion just as surely as a spoken consonant. This simple fact alone, Wagner wrote, should indicate that an orchestra has a far more varied language at its disposal than it has hitherto been given credit for. This was the factor that enabled it to participate closely and intimately in the drama itself. What now had to be considered was the relationship between the singers on stage and the instruments in the orchestra in presenting that drama.

Quite apart from the singer's acting ability, Wagner wrote, the purely sensual nature of his singing tone, with the infinite variety the juxtaposition of consonants and vowels lends to it, 'will be a much richer sound organ than any of the instruments in the orchestra. Not only that: it will also be a completely different sound organ, and it is this difference . . . that will determine once and for all what the attitude of the orchestra towards the actor-singer must be. Its first function is to demonstrate that the single note, then the whole melody and the singer's characterisation of it are fully in line with the requirements of musical harmony.' The orchestra achieves this by pursuing an independent musical line that, while supporting the singer harmonically, is at the same time making a statement on its own account. There should never be any attempt at a complete blend with the singer's tone. In Wagner's view it was this mistaken attempt that had led, in traditional opera, to singers being given melodies that were in fact purely instrumental in character, thus ensuring that they were sung and listened to for their sensuous qualities alone, without regard to the meaning of the words.

At this point Wagner resorted again to metaphor in an attempt to make his meaning clearer, and once again he chose water as his medium, comparing the dramatic singer's vocal line to an open boat on the clear waters of a mountain lake (the orchestra): 'The boat is an object completely different from the surface of the lake, yet it has been carpentered and equipped exclusively for use on water and with full regard to the characteristics of water. On land the open boat is completely useless, except at best, reduced to common planks, as firewood for the domestic cooking-stove. Only on the lake does it become something blissfully alive, cradled yet moving, in motion yet always at rest . . . But the boat is not hovering over the surface of the water: the lake can only carry it in a certain direction when the boat immerses the outer side of its body in the water. A thin piece of board that touches only the very surface of the lake will be tossed aimlessly around by the waves, while a clumsy stone will just sink to the bottom. But it is not only its outer body that the boat immerses in the water; it also immerses the tiller, which will decide the direction to be taken, and the oars, which will propel the boat in the chosen direction. Both of these, tiller and oars, draw their power to direct and to propel from their contact with the water, and it is the effective pressure of the guiding hand that makes it possible. With each forward-driving stroke the oars cut deep into the sounding surface of the water, and when they are raised, the water runs back in melodic drops from their wet blades.' Wagner's satisfaction with his metaphor was shown in his summing-up: 'It is not necessary for me to interpret this parable further in order to clarify my view of the degree of contact between the word and tone melody of the human voice and the orchestra, for in it this degree is fully indicated, as we will see even more clearly if we define operatic melody in the form we now know it as a musician's fruitless attempt to build a watertight boat out of the waves of the lake themselves.'

Having now established the orchestra as a participant in the drama of its own right with an independent identity of its own, Wagner set out to examine the precise nature of its contribution, which he defined at the outset as the power to express what cannot be expressed in words. This is of course the basic definition of absolute music, but, when applied to drama, it differs significantly in that the 'inexpressible' is not just theoretical, but actual. He had already pointed out the ability of a musical instrument, by virtue of its tonal colour, to speak directly to the emotions as no spoken word can, and in this way it could be used specifically to 'express' the inexpressible word. And it could also be applied to gesture – not just those involuntary physical movements we make at moments of heightened emotion, but also the unseen gesture which accompanies something thought but not spoken. In this capacity the orchestra's ability to express the unspoken might be seen simply as a useful aid to the actor-singers, but Wagner's ambition for it went much further than that, and it involved him in an analysis of the nature of thought itself. Put simply and briefly, his conclusion was that thought was the result of memory, and the emotions aroused by an object at first sight remained attached to it in the memory.

'The poet's verse now realises the thought, that is to say, he transforms a remembered, non-present feeling into a present, immediately perceptible feeling.' It is, however, only a described – and therefore a remote – feeling, but it gives rise to the composer's melody, which realises it anew, and in a form that enables all who hear it to perceive and to share its emotional impact to the same extent as the figure in the drama who is imparting it to us. This figure, as the drama progresses and other more immediate emotions take possession of him, will be aware of the previous emotion only as a memory, whereas we, the onlookers, are able to retain it in our minds in its purely melodic form. 'It has become a part of pure music, and, conveyed with suitable expression to our senses by the orchestra, it will appear to us as the realisation and actualisation of what was present only in the figure's thoughts . . . Even at moments when the actor addressing us seems no longer conscious of that particular emotion, the characteristic sound of the melody attached to it would, when heard in the orchestra, suggest to our thought connections and motives that have not yet found clear expression in the drama itself. In our own minds it would be, not just a thought, but the actualised emotional content of the thought.'

Here we see the birth of the concept that was to govern Wagner's compositional method for the rest of his life: the short melodic phrase which could be identified with a person, an emotion, a state of Nature, an action (to mention only a few of the various uses to which Wagner put such phrases in his subsequent works), and which provided the musical material out of which the whole score then evolved. A phrase of this kind has come to be known generally as a '*Leitmotiv*', though Wagner did not approve of the word. In *Opera and Drama* he referred to it initially as a '*Melodie*' and later just as a '*Motiv*'.

43

The identity of the idea or emotion contained in each such motive must be clearly established at its first appearance, otherwise the significance of its repetition will not be grasped. This can be done only through the poet's words. 'On its recurrence it [the musical motive] conveys a definite emotion to us, reminding us of the emotion which the figure, now in the grip of a new emotion arising out of it, leaves unspoken. Through the orchestra our senses are made aware of it . . . Our feelings become the enlightened witness of the organic growth of one emotion out of another, and in this way our feelings are given the power of thought, which in this context means something even higher than thought: the intuitive awareness of the thought contained within the emotion.'

The orchestra, Wagner recognised, had always possessed the power to anticipate, that is to say, to set the scene and prepare us emotionally for what is to come. He now investigated how this power could best be applied in the service of drama. Tone-painting – or as we more prosaically tend to call it, programme music – had so far been addressed mainly to the imagination and was in consequence somewhat cold and cerebral, but he saw no reason why it could not be aimed directly at the emotions. Indeed, in drama it was essential that it should be. Audiences must be prepared for what they are about to see, and to ensure that what is finally revealed to them proves convincing, it must coincide with their expectations. 'The actual appearance will then come to us as a desire fulfilled, an expectation confirmed; and when we remind ourselves that the poet, in order to affect our feelings, was obliged to present his images as mysterious and transcending ordinary life, we should also realise that these images could not reveal themselves to us thus, or they would at any rate remain unconvincing and alien, if their final naked appearance had not been preceded by a conditioning of our feelings and intuitions in a way that made them seem the inevitable and necessary response to our expectations. The tone language of the orchestra, inspired by the words of the poet, is the only medium that can arouse in us this necessary mood of expectation, and without its artistic aid the ideal drama can be neither conceived nor effected.'

With its powers of conveying immediate emotions, recalling past and anticipating future emotions, the orchestra, Wagner concluded, had taken over the commentatory role of the chorus in Greek tragedy. 'Let us now examine how the poet, from his place in the orchestra, through which he has been transformed into a complete musician, turns his attention back to the poetic aim that has led him thus far, in order to judge how to bring it finally to fruition with the enormously rich means he now has at his disposal.'

Drama, Wagner declared, differed from all other arts in that it presents, not something completed, but something in the actual process of completion. It consists of a series of situations, each giving rise to the next through the clash of individual personalities. The dramatist's first care must be to avoid leaving any traces of his creative manipulations, since the drama, if it is to take complete possession of our feelings, must develop inevitably, but unobtrusively, out of its confrontations. The first point of contact between the poet and his audience is at the level of a situation recognisable in ordinary life, since interest is aroused only when the events and personalities with which the drama deals are introduced in circumstances that are not so alien that they impede understanding. This interest once established, the manner in which the participants express themselves must be raised from the ordinary to the heightened.

The orchestra prepares the way by setting the mood of the drama about to be unfolded. 'It stirs and guides our feelings in the direction required by the poetic aim, arousing in us a mood of anticipation that only the appearance before our eyes of the expected object can satisfy. Should the poet now introduce this object in the form of a dramatic character, it would wound and disappoint our raised feelings if this character were to announce himself in language that would at once drag us back to the humdrum living surroundings from which we had just been transported. He must address us at the same level of language that originally [through the orchestra] had roused our feelings, thus identifying himself as part of that which we have been expecting . . . And he must speak in a way that will act upon our roused feelings. Our feelings can be influenced, however, only if they are given something to hold on to, a firm point around which they can gather in human sympathy and solidify into a special interest in this one particular human being who finds himself in this particular situation, is influenced by these particular surroundings, is inspired by this particular desire and is acting in this particular way. Such aspects, necessary to make the character of the individual clear to our feelings, can be explained convincingly only through words, in the same language that is involuntarily understood in real life . . . Our roused feelings have already insisted that the word language should match and be merged with the heightened level the orchestral language has led us to expect – the interpreter, as it were, as well as the sharer of these feelings – and from that it will logically follow that the content of what the figure in the drama is conveying to us will transcend ordinary life as surely as its expression transcends ordinary speech. The poet has only to remain true to his chosen form of expression, and to take care that the content of his drama is worthy of it, to see how far he has come towards the realisation of his aim, merely by paying close attention to the means of expression.'

At those points in the drama where words are necessary to move the action forward and the musical content is accordingly reduced, it is the orchestra, with its power of comment, that maintains the emotional temperature, and thus it plays a vital part in creating a unity of dramatic form. In traditional opera, Wagner maintained, no musical form existed outside the confines of each aria or other set vocal piece, except perhaps for a loose thematic connection that the composer had sought to establish in the overture. In his ideal drama, in which the music lends emotional force to the words, and the words articulate the music, the orchestra, by reminding and anticipating, by recalling past associations and expressing unspoken thoughts and feelings through its store of musical motives, is itself the unifying factor that creates and sustains an overall dramatic form. 'The main motives of the dramatic action, formed of significant melodic phrases each easily distinguishable from one another, create through constant and deliberate repetition (similar to that of rhyme) a unity of form that applies, not just to narrower sections, but also to the drama as a whole. They provide a close-knit structure within which the melodic phrases themselves function as mutually explanatory and therefore homogeneous. In addition, the emotions or insights contained in these phrases . . . are revealed to feeling as complementary and thus, according to their nature, uniform. With this close-knit structure a complete unity of form is effectively achieved.'

There *Opera and Drama* ends as far as technical matters are concerned, though Wagner did go on to express his feeling that it would be difficult to realise his ideas on the relationship between words and music in any language but German, which alone of the three traditional operatic languages (the others being Italian and French) was based directly on primal word roots. As regards the mutual responsibilities of poet and composer, he saw no reason why these should not be two separate persons, his one provision being that the composer should be 'younger in spirit' than the poet, a curious view to which I shall return in the next chapter. This chapter can most fittingly conclude with Wagner's own words, which appear towards the end of *Opera and Drama*: 'Whoever considers it to have been my intention here to set up an arbitrarily evolved system which musician and poet should follow from this moment on has made no effort to understand me. And whoever believes that anything new I might have said is based entirely on assumption, having nothing to do with experience and the nature of the subject under discussion, will not, even if he is willing, be in a position to understand me. What may seem new in what I have said is simply that unperceived element in the nature of the thing of which I have now become aware, and I became aware of it when, as a thinking artist, I grasped the connection between things that had hitherto been regarded by artists only in isolation. So I have invented nothing new: I have simply discovered that connection.'

Pursuing the Goal:

Opera and Drama in Practice

The first fruits of his 'painful expedition into the realms of speculative theory', as Wagner described *Opera and Drama* in his later essay 'Music of the Future' ('*Zukunftsmusik*', 1860), were, as I mentioned in the previous chapter, the completion of the text of *Der Ring des Nibelungen*. Yet not even this can be seen as the conscious carrying out of a plan worked out in advance. The text of *Siegfrieds Tod* had already been written, as we know, and the next to be written was *Der junge Siegfried*. It was begun in May 1851, only three months after the completion of *Opera and Drama*, and it was conceived as a self-contained drama, one that would indeed prepare the way for *Siegfrieds Tod*, but each work would be totally independent of the other. Wagner had even got to the stage of sketching out some of the music before he became conscious, as he explained in a letter to Liszt dated 20 November 1851, of 'a strange feeling of unease', the reason for which took him some time and thought to identify. Only then did he realise that *Der junge Siegfried* was not self-contained at all, but was a fragment of a larger drama: 'My inner conviction now tells me that a work of art – and that certainly includes the drama – can make its proper effect only when the poetic aim is conveyed fully, in all its important aspects, to the senses, and I least of all can now be permitted to sin against a truth, the validity of which I have recognised. So I must depict my whole myth in all its deepest and widest significance,

49

and that with the utmost artistic clarity, in order to be fully understood.'

In this same letter he indicated the proposed content of both *Das Rheingold* and *Die Walküre*, and his reason for writing the texts in reverse order may simply have been that he saw *Das Rheingold* as an extended introduction to the whole cycle rather than a work on its own, and introductions are often best left till last. That essential beginning to the drama which, as Wagner had written in *Opera and Drama*, it was the poet's first task to find, proved to be identical with the beginning of the prose sketch, 'The Nibelung Myth as Sketch for a Drama' ('*Der Nibelungen-Mythus als Entwurf zu einem Drama*'), which he had written in 1848 before starting work on *Siegfrieds Tod*.

The sketch, however, was not rigidly followed. In the course of the *Ring*'s development the whole balance of the action changed: Wotan joined Brünnhilde and Siegfried as the main protagonists, and, in place of the original idea of forgiveness and a happy reunion of all three in Valhalla, Wagner gave us the story of a god who, to atone for his crime, wills his own end. This suggests that unconscious dissatisfaction with the content as outlined in the sketch might have been a barrier to the work's progress, rather than the mere difficulty of establishing the right point at which to begin. Wagner's own explanation for the change of direction seems to bear this contention out. It is contained in a letter to his friend August Röckel dated 23 August 1856, well after the completion of the final text of the *Ring*: 'The period during which I worked in obedience to my intuitions dated from *Der Fliegende Holländer*. *Tannhäuser* and *Lohengrin* followed and, if there is any expression of an underlying poetic motive in these works, it is to be sought in the sublime tragedy of renunciation, the negation of the will, which here appears as necessary and inevitable, and alone capable of bringing about redemption. It was this deep underlying idea which gave my poetry and music that peculiar aura without which they would not have the power to move people so profoundly. Now, the strange thing is that, in all my intellectual ideas on life and in all the concepts I had arrived at in my struggles to understand the world with my conscious reason, I was working in direct opposition to the intuitive ideas expressed in these works. My most remarkable discovery in this respect concerned my *Nibelungen* drama. It had taken form at a time when, with my intellect, I had built up for myself an optimistic world based on Hellenic principles. I believed that, in order to realise such a world, it was only necessary for mankind to wish it. The problem of why they did *not* seem to wish it I tried somewhat elaborately to circumvent. It was with this definite creative purpose that I conceived the character of Siegfried, as the representation of an existence freed from suffering. But I hoped to make my meaning even clearer in the depiction of the Nibelung myth as a whole – by describing the first act of wrongdoing, from which a whole world of evil arose. This world had to fall to pieces in order to teach us how to recognise evil, to tear it up by the roots and erect a juster world in its place. I was scarcely aware that, in working out my scheme, I was being unconsciously guided by a completely different intuition, infinitely more profound: instead of depicting a phase in the evolution of the world, I had indeed grasped the nature of life itself in all its possible phases and had recognised its nothingness. The consequence of that was – since I held to my intuitions and not to my abstract ideas – that something quite different emerged from what I had originally intended.'

The extent to which Wagner's intuitions both influenced and were influenced by his abstract ideas is vividly illustrated in *Opera and Drama* by his interpretation of the Oedipus legend in the light of his conclusions (heavily guided by the philosophy of Ludwig Feuerbach) on the relationship between individual will and state law. Wagner's analysis contains so many ideas and situations present in the full text of the *Ring* but not to be found in the 'Nibelung Myth' sketch, that one must see it as a preliminary working-out, whether conscious or not, of the new theme underlying the tetralogy.

One can hardly doubt that Oedipus's encounter with his unrecognised father Laius suggested Siegfried's meeting with his unrecognised grandfather Wotan in the third act of *Siegfried*, nor that the incest which led to the downfall of Oedipus and Jocasta was in Wagner's mind as he dealt with Siegmund and Sieglinde in *Die Walküre*. The gist of Wagner's remarks in *Opera and Drama* concerning the morality of incest can be found in essence in the argument between Wotan and Fricka in the second act of that work. The warring brothers Eteocles and Polynices must have given Wagner the idea for the clash between Fafner and Fasolt, which does not figure in the 'Nibelung Myth' sketch. In the *Ring* this clash serves a similar purpose: to demonstrate the evil of possessions. In Wotan in his guise of Wanderer we can see clear traces of Creon, the 'wise' political manipulator, setting people against each other for his own advantage. Wotan had already been Laius, not only in his encounter with Siegfried, but also as the perpetrator of the crime – a different one, admittedly – that set the whole vast drama in motion. And it may not be too rash to claim that, in his confrontation in the third act of *Siegfried* with Erda, Wotan briefly became Oedipus himself answering the Pythia. Wagner wrote to King Ludwig of Bavaria on 24 February 1869, as he started work on that scene: 'Here, like the ancient Greeks in the steaming caverns of Delphi, we come to the centre of the great cosmic tragedy. A world is coming to its end: the god is striving for its rebirth, for he is the world's will. Everything here is sublime foreboding, expressible only in riddles.'

However, it would be absurd to suggest that in his *Ring* tetralogy Wagner simply set out to provide a German imitation of the Oedipus legend. The inexact and overlapping parallels I have indicated are proof in themselves that no such thought existed in Wagner's mind. The situation may rather have been this: in his reflections on just why myth possessed the power to appeal to all the senses at one and the same time, Wagner chose the Oedipus story to illustrate the arguments he had put forward regarding the effects of myth on both the conscious and the unconscious mind. His interpretation of it was therefore influenced by the subject that was occupying him – probably more subconsciously than consciously – at the time of writing, that is to say, the Siegfried saga. That the two should have intertwined – one influencing or being influenced by the other at certain points and in certain situations – is in these circumstances not surprising.

It may be fair to assume a more conscious process at work in the virtual identification of Brünnhilde with Antigone, not only in their devotion to their respective fathers, but also in their decisive acts when left to their own devices. Brünnhilde as Wagner had already depicted her in *Siegfrieds Tod* was a far lesser figure than she subsequently became in the *Ring* cycle. Essentially in *Siegfrieds Tod* she remained Wotan's devoted and subservient daughter. In *Die Walküre* she displays the same selfless love that Antigone feels for her disgraced brother Polynices, the love best defined by the biblical expression 'charity', as she attempts to save Siegmund in defiance of Wotan's command to let him die – a command as politically inspired as Creon's concerning the disposal of Polynices's body.

The final text of *Der Ring des Nibelungen*, which included some adaptation of *Der junge Siegfried* and of *Siegfrieds Tod*, was finished by the end of 1852. Though in the course of the following year Wagner jotted down various musical themes, it was not until September that, as he related in a famous passage in his autobiography *My Life* (*Mein Leben*), he awoke in La Spezia (Italy) from a doze and 'realised that the orchestral prelude to *Das Rheingold*, which I had been carrying around inside me but had been unable to locate precisely, had at last emerged.'

What had emerged was not so much the music itself, but the means of moving it forward. Though he had written at length in *Opera and Drama* of the dramatic significance of key changes and modulation, he had not apparently considered from a purely practical viewpoint the mechanics of making a start. Having in his reflections in *Opera and Drama* identified a close tie between dramatic action and musical modulation, Wagner found himself faced in practice with the problem of what to do when no dramatic action has yet taken place. The solution that came to him in his dreamlike state in La Spezia was the bold one of holding on to the chord of E flat major for a full five minutes, relying entirely on arpeggio accelerations and instrumental colourations to avoid monotony as he evokes the depths of a great river in an unspoiled natural world. It is not until some time after the curtain rises and the happy frolickings of the three Rhinemaidens are interrupted by the lustful dwarf Alberich that modulation enters to exert its dramatic influence. Once started, the store of melodic motives arising from each developing situation – and from then on associated with it in our minds – began to build up, providing the composer with an increasingly rich supply of material for the commentary on the action which he had identified as one of the dramatic functions of the orchestra. Within a very short stage time, judged in relation to the drama as a whole, he was able to carry us down from the gods on the mountain tops to the dwarfs in the depths of the earth with a powerful orchestral interlude based on a variety of motives old and new and utilising to the full his remarkable command of instrumental sound colour.

Both orchestral pieces, the introduction and the descent into Nibelheim, are outstanding examples of music's power to induce in us an emotional state in which we can accept without question the '*Wunder*' of which Wagner wrote: the sight of a dwarf breathing under water and fashioning from stolen gold magic trinkets promising world power. There are many such moments of *Wunder* throughout the *Ring*, and they differ in kind from the *Wunder* of the earlier works. The heroes of these – a spectral sailor, a poet who has enjoyed the sexual favours of a goddess and a knight from the mystical land of Monsalvat – belong to the world of fantasy too, but in all three cases the fantasy is a precondition of the dramatic action, not an active part of it: the various dilemmas of the Dutchman, Tannhäuser and Lohengrin are dealt with in purely human terms without the help of those supernatural devices that Wagner used, as dramatic short cuts, throughout the *Ring*, with its intermingling of gods, giants, dwarfs, water spirits and human beings, and again in *Tristan und Isolde*, with its love potion. When such objects as love potions, helmets providing invisibility, magic swords and talking birds are introduced, he always contrives through the emotional force of his music to keep our feelings beyond the reach of the cold light of reason.

Orchestral introductions, Wagner saw, had a major part to play in evoking this heightened state of the emotions, and here lay his main reason for abandoning the initial overture, which – mistakenly in his view – attempted to summarise the whole content of the drama before it had even begun. The storm of *Die Walküre*, he declared in his essay 'On the Application of Music to the Drama' ('*Über die Anwendung der Musik auf das Drama*', 1879), and the smithy sounds of *Siegfried* contain the elements of the drama to come. 'The introduction to the Norns' scene in *Götterdämmerung* called, however, for a different approach: here the fates of the primeval world are being wound into a silken thread that on the rising of the curtain we must see swinging between the three sombre sisters if we are to understand its meaning. For that reason the orchestral introduction before the curtain rises had to be kept short and tight, but, through the use of motives whose meanings were clear from earlier parts of the work, a richer harmonic and thematic treatment became possible.'

In the first three parts of the *Ring* Wagner observed his dictum of starting the stage action 'at the level of a situation recognisable in ordinary life': Alberich's incongruous wooing of the three Rhinemaidens (never mind if under water!), Siegmund's storm-driven arrival in Hunding's house, Mime's frustrated efforts in his cave to forge a sword – these are situations that at once arouse understanding and curiosity. The sight of three strange female figures swinging a silken rope and exchanging cryptic words does not. Of course, if the *Ring* is regarded as a single work, *Götterdämmerung* is not in itself a beginning, and our initial interest can therefore be assumed as already engaged. Yet its original version, *Siegfrieds Tod*, which was designed to stand alone as a drama, began in exactly the same way with the three Norns, whose words seem even more cryptic, when they come on us straight from the blue. It is another indication of Wagner's error in having unwittingly begun his drama somewhere past the middle, an

error he was eventually led by *Opera and Drama* to recognise
and put right by creating the preceding parts that placed it
where it belonged in the drama as a whole.

His promotion of the orchestra from the role of mere
accompanist to that of commentator caused him, as we have
seen, to rethink the function of the choristers on stage and to
treat them as individuals participating directly in the drama,
even when appearing only in groups. The first beneficiaries
of this innovation were the Valkyries, to each of whom
in *Die Walküre* Wagner gave names as well as individual
snatches of dialogue. In *Siegfrieds Tod* they were to have
come to Brünnhilde on the rock to which she had been
banished to commiserate with her on her downfall, and to
have sung *en bloc* in formal words strongly reminiscent of
Greek tragedy. In the corresponding scene in *Götterdämmerung*
the entire sisterhood was replaced, to its great advantage in
regard to both dramatic tension and emotional impact, by
the single figure of Waltraute.

In the *Ring* there is no choral singing in the traditional sense
before the second act of *Götterdämmerung*, when Hagen calls
the Gibichungs together to celebrate Gunther's wedding.
This act in particular has retained much of the traditional
operatic shape from which Wagner had not yet freed himself
at the time the text of *Siegfrieds Tod* was written, and it is
surprising that he did not revise it more thoroughly when
he came to adapt it for use in *Götterdämmerung*. However, he
did add some touches to Hagen's scene in order to enable
the Gibichung men to preserve their individuality as far as
possible. They arrive gradually, singly to begin with, then
in twos and threes, and even when fully assembled, they
are divided for singing purposes into at least four groups,
each with differing words and melodic lines, and there is
also occasional use of a solo voice. Through devices such

as these Wagner established a dramatic motivation for his crowd scenes, thus turning the moment when the assembled people burst forth in unison from a convention into a natural expression of shared feelings.

His treatment of the chorus was similar in all his works following *Opera and Drama*, its use entirely dependent on dramatic motivation and dramatic effect. Where it had little or nothing to contribute, the chorus was confined just to a few isolated exclamations or reduced to the level of silent extras, as in *Tristan und Isolde*. In *Die Meistersinger von Nürnberg*, on the other hand, it came fully into its own, a collection of individuals, whether peacefully singing a chorale in church as in the first act, rioting in the streets as in the second, or frolicking on the festival meadow in the third. The uprising of the citizens of Nuremberg on Midsummer's Eve, that grand contrapuntal crescendo of voices spread over fourteen staves, each singing different words, might be placed beside the '*Wach auf*' chorus, their formal but heartfelt tribute to their revered cobbler-poet Hans Sachs next day on the festival meadow, as Wagner's triumphant demonstration of the huge dramatic range open to a chorus in the hands of a composer as alive to its possibilities as he was.

In the previous chapter I quoted a passage in *Opera and Drama* that seemed to point to *Tristan und Isolde*. There is another that points just as clearly to *Die Meistersinger*, and it occurs in the section in which Wagner was dealing with the conflict between individual instinct and community will in his analysis of the Oedipus legend. In fact, it has more to do with human than state relationships and is concerned in particular with the difference between youth and age: 'A person is not the same in youth as in old age: in our youth we long for deeds, in our old age for repose . . . The aged person's recompense for the gradual loss of his urge to act is *experience*, which can be enjoyable and instructive for the experienced person himself, but any attempt to influence the inexperienced person through it can succeed only if the young person's own urge to act is weak and he is easily led, or if the lesson to be learnt from that particular experience can be imposed on him as an obligatory guideline for his behaviour.'

However, experience could be put to a more fruitful use when it was inspired by love: 'A loving father knows that he has not yet experienced everything, that he can still vastly enrich himself by making the experiences of his beloved child his own. The beauty of repose in old age lies in the ability to take pleasure in the deeds of others, and through love to turn these into objects worthy of enjoyment and giving enjoyment to oneself. Such repose is the natural product of that kind of paternal love, and in no way does it hinder youth's urge to act – on the contrary, it encourages activity . . . Experienced old age is in a position to grasp the nature of youthful activities that are the unwitting consequence of instinctive urges, and it can see them in context. Since he can consciously define and explain them, a man of experience can justify these activities more completely than the youthful doer himself. In the repose of old age we attain the highest point of poetic ability, and a man striving to acquire a similar judicious attitude towards the phenomena of life must first win that repose. Experience's loving admonition to inexperience . . . achieves its most convincing and successful results through providing the instinctive doer with an accurate picture of his own nature. A young man swept along in an unconscious lust for living will not be brought to a judicious awareness of his own nature through moral injunctions: that aim can be achieved with full success only by enabling him to look on a true picture of himself, for true cognition is recognition, just as true consciousness is an awareness of the unconscious inside us.'

This is the idea that lies behind the relationship between Hans Sachs and Walther von Stolzing as shown in Wagner's comedy, just as the clash between the hidebound master-singers and the natural instinctiveness of the common folk is a reflection of his views on the corporate state and the individual. *Die Meistersinger* had been conceived in 1845, the year in which *Tannhäuser* was first staged, and it was intended, as Wagner told us in *My Life*, as a satirical comment on that work. The synopsis he wrote down in 1845 did not contain the scene in which the elderly cobbler-poet coaxes the impulsive young knight through the composition of his Prize Song. In that early sketch Sachs is not the warmly human father figure he finally became, but a disappointed and embittered old man. It seems more than likely that Wagner's musings on youth and age in *Opera and Drama* had a mellowing effect on his satire when it eventually came to be written – at a time when he was in any case closer in years to Hans Sachs than to the impetuous Walther von Stolzing.

The difference between age and youth, experience and inexperience cropped up again in the concluding pages of *Opera and Drama*. Wagner was addressing the question whether poet and musician should be two persons or one, and he wrote: 'The poet and the musician we have in mind could quite easily be two persons. In fact, the poet might very well feel that the musician, since he forms the practical link between the poetic aim and its final physical realisation on stage, ought to be a separate person, and one younger than the poet, not necessarily in age, but certainly in character. This younger person, standing closer to the life of the instincts, including its lyrical aspects, might seem to the more experienced and reflective poet better fitted to realise his aim than he himself, and his natural affection for his younger and more excitable colleague would, in the moment the musician enthusiastically took to himself the poetic aim imparted to him by the older man, blossom into that fine and noble love that we have seen to be the motivating force of a work of art.'

Since Wagner was insolubly his own poet, this idea amounts to hardly more than a speculation – no doubt kindly meant – for the benefit of less widely talented poets and musicians than he himself was. All the same, it is interesting for the emphasis it places on the poet as the leading partner in music drama. For this apparent bias he was widely criticised when *Opera and Drama* first appeared. 'I know what Nietzsche didn't like in it,' he told Cosima on 11 February 1872. 'It is the same thing which [Ernst] Kossak took up and which set Schopenhauer against me: what I said about words. At the time I didn't dare to say that it was music which produced drama, although inside myself I knew it.' His remark was nonsense, of course, for who would have objected to Wagner adopting a view that was already generally held – the view that in opera the music is more important than the words? In fact, in *Opera and Drama* the question of absolute predominance never directly arose. If in the course of his argument the balance tended now this way, now that, it was always in relation to the dramatic content: there were times when words took the lead, others when music held sway. In effect there was always only a single dominant factor: the drama itself.

A general comparison between the three works that arose directly from the ideas expressed in *Opera and Drama* must place the *Ring* in the centre as the work in which the drama uses words and music in equal measure as the driving force, with *Tristan* on one side as propelled mainly by music and *Die Meistersinger* on the other as propelled mainly by words. This is a view that Wagner himself took in regard to *Tristan*, as Cosima recorded in her diary on 1 October 1878: 'R. talks again of his need at that time to push himself to the limits musically, since in the *Nibelungen* the requirements of the drama frequently forced him to restrict the musical expression.'

If, then, the desire to 'push himself to the limits musically' was Wagner's main incentive for setting the *Ring* aside in the middle of *Siegfried* in order to write *Tristan*, it is reasonable to assume that his frustrations in connection with the staging of *Tristan* and the failure of his revised *Tannhäuser* in Paris were the main causes of his seeking refuge, after those two disappointments, in the less intense, more mundane world of comedy. Dealing as it does with the actions of real people in a real world, comedy uses words in a factual way, and the contrast could hardly be greater than that between the ejaculatory emotional outpourings of the *Tristan* text and the everyday speech of the characters in *Die Meistersinger*. There is also much more variety of action and of character in *Die Meistersinger*, as well as extended scenes in which a clear understanding of the words is essential: the scenes, for example, in which Sachs's apprentice David explains the rules of the mastersingers to Walther von Stolzing, and Sachs helps Walther with the composition of his Prize Song.

Much of *Tristan* is written in the alliterative verse so strongly advocated in *Opera and Drama*; this time, however, with a sprinkling of those end rhymes which in his book he had somewhat scornfully dismissed. *Die Meistersinger* is cast entirely in rhyming couplets of the kind the historic poet Hans Sachs himself used. In both works the music is based firmly on the principles he had laid down for the *Ring*, that is to say, it is built up on a series of leading motives closely associated with individual aspects of the drama.

When he came to write *Tristan* Wagner, with *Das Rheingold*,

Die Walküre and two acts of *Siegfried* behind him, was in full command of this musical technique. In it he created a work that, as he declared in his essay 'Music of the Future', could be judged 'according to the strictest demands based on my theories – not because I wrote it to any system – by this time I had completely forgotten all theory – but because here at last I was able to proceed with such complete freedom and disregard of all theoretical considerations that while writing it I was myself aware that I was going far beyond my own system.'★

Going beyond it indeed, but not in the sense of rejecting it: from the point of view of drama pure and simple, *Tristan und Isolde* is the most uncompromising expression of Wagner's ideas, the prelude securely fulfilling its anticipatory function and raising our emotions to respond to the situation we see on curtain rise, a situation 'at the level of ordinary life' – essentially the forcing of a helpless maiden into a marriage of convenience – that can immediately engage our sympathies. The manner in which Wagner, from that starting point, proceeds to lead our attention away from outward events to the conflicts within the two lovers themselves, so that we, like them, see the outer world as something unreal and obtrusive – this is a model of the concentration and singleness of purpose laid down in *Opera and Drama* as essential ingredients of the ideal drama, and one that triumphantly demonstrates the wisdom of his warning to the dramatist to avoid leaving any traces of his creative manipulations.

At first sight *Die Meistersinger* seems deliberately to challenge the need for any such conformity. Wagner begins the work with an overture, a form he had castigated in his book

★ Translation by Robert L. Jacobs

as a sign of the composer's vanity. In his score he called his opening piece a *Vorspiel* (prelude), but in *My Life* he gave it its true title of overture and – another transgression against his theory – claimed to have conceived the main part of it 'with the utmost clarity' before there was anything more in his mind than the bare story he had sketched out sixteen years previously. The extended musical themes of this overture, ostensibly conceived as absolute music, might seem at first hearing to be far removed in character from the short melodic phrases out of which the *Ring* and *Tristan* had been built. In fact, divided up, they yielded a large number of motives that Wagner could play with in order to set the action in motion. The chorale the congregation is singing as the curtain rises, for instance, is based on the motive for the mastersingers with which the overture begins.

Die Meistersinger also differs from the other works in that it contains a number of set solo pieces – one hesitates to call them arias – to which the action naturally gives rise. In the first act there is Pogner's announcement of his decision to give his daughter in marriage to the winner of a song competition, as well as Walther's two trial songs, '*Am stillen Herd*' and '*Fanget an!*'. Each of these, while impeccably motivated from a dramatic point of view, is a melody in its own right, but it is also more: the source of further motives on which Sachs draws profusely in his *Flieder* monologue in the second act. Sachs's third act *Wahn* monologue, for which the orchestral introduction and the gentle comedy with his apprentice David so exquisitely prepare us, is again compounded of motives already familiar, together with the sad new mood of resignation signalled in the introduction, which tells us that Sachs is feeling his years. The scene is now set for the deployment of the work's central theme of youth and age, innovation and tradition, as in a fatherly way Sachs leads Walther along the difficult path of conscious artistic creation without seeming to impose his own influence.

To celebrate the completion of the Prize Song, Wagner reverted to a traditional operatic form of which he had made no use since *Lohengrin*: the ensemble of principal singers. That quintet, and the scene on the festival meadow that follows it, with its choruses, its dances and its two fully-fledged arias (Walther's Prize Song and Sachs's '*Verachtet mir die Meister nicht*') might be described as sheer traditional opera. Does this mean therefore that, when creating a realistic comedy, Wagner found it necessary to abandon the dramatic ideas he had formulated in *Opera and Drama*, or at least some of them?

On the contrary: each of the ingredients in the last scene is just as firmly motivated, and as emotionally compelling in words and music, as all that precedes it, both in this and the other works written after he had consciously examined and defined them in his book. *Die Meistersinger von Nürnberg* is not an exception, but a convincing demonstration of the validity of those ideas and of their relevance to dramatic works of all kinds.

In 'Music of the Future', in which he briefly summarised for the benefit of the French public ideas expressed in *Opera and Drama*, Wagner spoke rather disparagingly of his book, claiming that it was written at a time when his brain was 'strangely and morbidly depressed', and he observed, 'I cannot but suppose that its minutely detailed exposition of my main thought must have been more interesting to myself than it could ever be to others, either now or in the future.'* But

---

* Translation by Robert L. Jacobs

at no time did he disclaim the thoughts themselves. 'I talk a lot with R. about *Opera and Drama*,' Cosima wrote in her diary on 12 August 1878. 'He opens the book and, reading a point in it, recognises with pleasure the unity of his whole life and work.'

The One and Indivisible Art:
The Reason for Bayreuth

The erection of a theatre for his music dramas was not mere vanity, but an integral part of Wagner's attempt, as significant to him as the dramas themselves, to convince the world that art is one of the profoundest influences in the world and, as such, must be approached both reverently and responsibly. Considering himself to be first and foremost a dramatist, he was fully aware of the vital importance of the place in which his work was presented. Time and time again he voiced the opinion that a drama could not be said to exist until it was performed, and for him a bad or an inadequate performance was the equivalent of, perhaps even worse than, no performance at all.

The musical theatre to which Wagner committed himself in 1833, when at the age of twenty he accepted a post as chorus master and occasional conductor in Würzburg, was one he basically despised. Beginning (like virtually all great dramatists) at the practical end of his art, he was initially more concerned to establish himself than to proselytise, though he had already received a vivid impression of what the musical theatre could achieve when, four years earlier in Leipzig, he had seen Wilhelmine Schröder-Devrient playing in *Fidelio*. As he tells us in his autobiography *My Life*, he immediately wrote the great singer a letter 'in which I briefly told her that from that moment my life had acquired its true significance, and that if in days to come she should ever hear my name praised in the world of art she must remember that she had that evening made me what I then swore it was my destiny to become.'

In the pursuit of his destiny it can be doubted whether the six years of his apprenticeship in Würzburg, Magdeburg and Riga did much more than merely confirm his view that the modern operatic stage was basically frivolous, though they did provide him with an opportunity of developing his composing craft: *Die Feen* and *Das Liebesverbot* were completed and *Rienzi* begun in this period. And impressions of all kinds were being registered along the way, the ultimate significance of which were perhaps not immediately recognised, but were later to be remembered and acted on. It was, for instance, in the little theatre in Riga that Wagner first realised that the shape and atmosphere of an auditorium can greatly influence the impact of a performance. The seats in the theatre at Riga were steeply raked, the auditorium was dark and the orchestra was placed low before the stage, almost out of sight of the audience. The lessons to be learnt from that were not forgotten.

Two years later, in Paris, where he next went in his search for fame, Wagner made another interesting technical discovery. Arriving late at the Conservatoire to hear Habeneck rehearsing a Beethoven symphony, he was put in a room divided from the main concert hall by a partition stopping short of the ceiling. As he recalled to his friend Felix Dräseke twenty years later, the sound of the orchestra reaching him over the partition amazed him: the music, freed of all mechanical side effects, 'came to the ear in a compact and ethereal sort of unity.'

Such reminiscences, written down years later when their relevance to the theatre eventually built in Bayreuth was clearly apparent, must of course be treated with some reserve.

Certainly they cannot be taken as evidence that Wagner at this early period of his life was definitely thinking of one day building a theatre of his own. All the same, there can be no reason to doubt that the impressions were registered and went, along with Wilhelmine Schröder-Devrient, into the storeroom of his mind for future, if still undefined, use.

More reliable evidence of the conscious progress of his thoughts as a young man can be found in the essays, short stories and journalistic reports that Wagner, thwarted in his attempts to gain a footing in the operatic world, wrote during his stay of two and a half years in Paris in order to gain a living. These provide a fascinating self-portrait, all the more revealing in that it is not always intended. One of the first pieces he wrote for the *Gazette musicale*, entitled 'On German Music' ('*Über deutsches Musikwesen*'), shows the depth of his national feeling. His analysis of the German spirit, naïve and over-idealistic as it is, accurately pinpoints the essential gods: Bach, Mozart, Beethoven, Weber. Their moral earnestness, their basic simplicity – scorning superficial brilliance – were the qualities on which German opera, should it ever flourish in its own right, ought to be based. In Mozart's *Die Zauberflöte* and Weber's *Der Freischütz* he discerned the essential qualities, and they were qualities for which French opera, for all its technical competence (and Wagner was sufficiently a professional to pay sincere tribute to that) had little use.

In another literary piece, the short story 'Death in Paris' ('*Ein Ende in Paris*'), Wagner portrayed an idealistic young German composer who, unable to compromise with Parisian musical convention, starves to death. These are among his dying words: 'I believe in God, Mozart and Beethoven, likewise in their disciples and apostles; I believe in the Holy Ghost and in the truth of the one and indivisible Art; I believe this Art to be an emanation of God that dwells in the hearts of all enlightened men; I believe that whoever has steeped himself in its holy joy must dedicate himself to it forever and can never deny it; I believe that all men are blessed through Art and that it is therefore permissible to die of hunger for its sake . . . I believe in a Day of Judgement upon which all who dared to exploit this chaste and noble Art for the sake of profit, and all who in the baseness of their hearts dishonoured and disgraced it for the sake of sensual pleasure will be fearfully punished.'*

It is an embryonic, still undirected expression of his own creed, but Wagner, being of stronger stuff than his own hero, knew in his heart that mere intentions are not enough. In another essay, 'The Artist and the Public' ('*Der Künstler und die Öffentlichkeit*'), he examined, admittedly in a somewhat confused and inconclusive way, the irresistible urge of the artist to communicate, even if in his longing to share his divine discoveries he runs the risk of desecrating them. 'It is then,' he wrote, 'that he allows himself to sup with the devil, giving himself the right because he knows, however many lies he may tell, that his truthfulness can never be sullied.'* It was in this practical spirit, confident of his ability to withdraw before it was too late, that Wagner wrote songs for reigning Parisian singers (though none of them was performed), and in this spirit too he wrote the libretto for a one-act opera which, since it could be used as a curtain-raiser, might win him a footing in the Paris Opéra. It did not, though the Opéra brought the libretto from him for setting by another composer.

Such was the origin of *Der Fliegende Holländer*. In spite of having sold his libretto, Wagner set about composing music to it himself, and what had been conceived as a curtain-raiser

* Translation by Robert L. Jacobs and Geoffrey Skelton

turned in his hands into a full-length opera. If Wagner, still in
the process of making discoveries, could have made one here
about his own character, he evidently did not do so, for he
was to repeat the same mistake on two more occasions during
his life: both with *Tristan und Isolde* and *Die Meistersinger von
Nürnberg* he set out to write popular and easily produceable
works to restore his immediate fortunes. It seems that some
force was at work inside him which in the end always held
him to his artistic convictions and refused to allow him to
carry out his own intended compromises. The devil with
whom he sometimes chose to sup could only, one is inclined
to conclude, have been his guardian angel in disguise!

Paris may have saved him from his rash willingness to
compromise by refusing to have anything to do with him on
any terms. Dresden, to which he went in 1842 as conductor,
provided a far severer test. Both *Rienzi* and *Der Fliegende
Holländer* had been accepted for production there. The first
was a great success, the second a partial failure. It would
have been easy for him, encouraged by his first wife Minna
and most of his friends, to draw the conclusion that he should
stay where he was and establish his position by writing more
operas like *Rienzi*. At least he would be assured of comfort
and respect, and the Dresden Opera, to which his idol
Wilhelmine Schröder-Devrient currently belonged, enjoyed
a good reputation. Could not his ambition of raising the
standards of German opera be achieved better there than
anywhere else?

The factor that spoke most strongly in Wagner's mind
against this argument was the lack of recognition for *Der
Fliegende Holländer*, a work he knew to contain far more of
his ultimate beliefs than the pompous and derivative *Rienzi*.
And his feelings of dissatisfaction were only inflamed by the
reception of *Tannhäuser*, which he had written in Dresden

in a spirit of isolation induced by the conflict inside him between his convictions and the temptations of material success. *Tannhäuser*, though it both expressed his artistic beliefs (to the best of his ability at the time) and pleased the public, was, he felt, appreciated for the wrong reasons – for its superficial beauties rather than for its moral message. The fact that Wagner himself had contributed to the misunderstanding by making damaging cuts in his work merely proved the difficulty of his self-imposed task. Opera, in Dresden as in Paris, was at the mercy of people – managers and singers (for whose sake the cuts had been made) – who cared for nothing except their own personal glory. What chance had a dramatist, musical or otherwise, of getting his message through to the audience under those circumstances?

It was the culmination of all these experiences and conclusions that led Wagner in 1849 to define, for the first time in writing, his ideas for the reform of the operatic stage. His study bore the title 'A Plan for the Organisation of a German National Theatre for the Kingdom of Saxony' ('*Entwurf zur Organisation eines deutschen National-Theaters für das Königreich Sachsen*') and was addressed, as Wagner tells us, to the members of parliament in Saxony, who were threatening at the time (revolution being in the air) to cut the subsidy of the existing court theatre. Wagner felt rather naïvely that to present a plan for a more democratically organised theatre would avert the threat by showing a way to establish the theatre on a broader social and a more genuinely artistic basis.

Reading his study now, one is struck both by its thoroughness and the practicality of its approach. It is obviously the work of a man who had learnt much from experience. In this essay he defined in great detail the terms under which singers and orchestral players should be engaged and what steps should be taken to train them – an interesting foreshadowing of later attempts in Munich and Bayreuth to do exactly that. But its most daring proposal was that the director of the theatre should no longer be appointed by the king, but should be democratically elected by a majority vote of the entire theatre personnel, together with members of a society of German authors and composers.

In this document there is no mention at all of theatre buildings as such. It is perhaps not altogether surprising, since Wagner was here concerned mainly with organisational matters. But one feels that, if he had at the time had any definite ideas on the importance of a theatre's shape, he would have found room in his study to define them – in the same way that he seized the opportunity to define his conception of the theatre's social function. 'In theatrical art,' he wrote, 'all forms of art combine to a greater or lesser extent to make an impression on the public such as none of the other arts can make in isolation. Its essential character is socialisation, while preserving in full all the rights of the individual.'

There is certainly a liberality about this last sentence more appealing than the dictum of Emperor Joseph II which the composer went on to quote with open approval: 'The theatre should have no other duty except to contribute to the elevation of taste and morals.' This on the face of it is sheer didacticism, and one feels that, had Wagner adhered to such a dictum in his own works, he would hardly have been the powerful artistic force he was later to become. His dramas themselves provide the best evidence that he was alive to the need in the theatre to entertain as well as to instruct. His basic complaint about the opera of his day was that it sought *only* to entertain – in other words, that it was trivial. He was profoundly convinced that the operatic form was capable of expressing eternal truths and had indeed already done so in the operas of Gluck, Mozart, Beethoven and Weber – even to some extent in such lesser works as Auber's *La Muette de Portici*, Halévy's *La Juive* and Spontini's *La Vestale*. The 'elevation of taste and morals' which he was seeking to secure applied in his own mind mainly to the managers and singers: only if they could be persuaded to approach their task in the proper exalted spirit would the moral influence on their audiences be effected. Wagner believed implicitly in the power of music, as well as words, to influence morals. 'We can maintain with some confidence,' he stated bravely in his 'Plan', 'that Beethoven enthusiasts are more active and energetic citizens than those under the spell of Rossini, Bellini and Donizetti: these are mere well-to-do and genteel idlers.'

In his vocabulary Wagner here borrowed something from the revolutionary socialists with whom he was associating at that time (1849), and it is not surprising that his proposals for a national theatre on co-operative lines were emphatically spurned by both court and parliament. He himself, as we know, was found guilty of taking part in the revolution and banished from Germany. This is not the place to examine the justice or otherwise of that decision, but it can surely be claimed, whatever rash statements and acts the composer might have been led into in those excitable days, that his thinking was never political in a strictly sociological sense. Fundamentally he was not out to sweep aside the King of Saxony, but simply the management of Saxony's main opera house.

The special nature of Wagner's socialism can be clearly seen in the long essay, 'Art and Revolution' (*'Die Kunst und die Revolution'*), which he wrote in Zurich in the year of his flight from Germany. Here for the first time he made use of the word *Gesamtkunstwerk*, though in a different sense from that in which it was later applied to the structure of his music dramas. He used it in relation to the drama of ancient Greece, which, he claimed, was an integral part of the social structure and not just a recreational excrescence. 'The theatre,' he wrote, re-echoing the claim expressed in his rejected 'Plan', 'is the most comprehensive, the most influential of all artistic institutions, and before human beings can freely practise their noblest activity, which is art, how can they hope to be free and independent in other, lower directions? Eternally youthful art, always able to refresh itself from the noblest spirits of its time, is better equipped than a senile religion that has lost its hold on the public, than an incapable government, to steer the turbulent currents of social movements past the wild cliffs and treacherous shallows towards their great and noble goal – the goal of true humanity.' In other words, liberate the theatre and the rest will follow of its own accord.

The revolutions of 1848–49 and his banishment from Germany were responsible for a radical change in Wagner's ideas on how to set about rescuing the human race through the theatre. Up to that point all his efforts had been directed towards reforming the existing operatic theatre from within – not only through his own works and those of his equally high-minded predecessors, but also by placing its management in more dedicated hands. Now he came to the drastic conclusion that the only way was to destroy the existing theatre and start again from the beginning.

Writing in September 1850 from Zurich to his friend and fellow revolutionary Theodor Uhlig, he speculated on how this might be done: 'Here on a nice meadow close to the town I would build a crude theatre of planks and beams according to my own design and furnish it simply with the machinery and decorations needed for a production of *Siegfried*. Then I would select the most suitable singers I could find and invite them to Zurich for six weeks. I would aim at forming a chorus mainly from volunteers (there are splendid voices and strong healthy people to be found here!), and I would get my orchestra together in the same way. In the New Year, announcements would be published in all German newspapers, inviting all friends of the music drama to my dramatic music festival. Everyone coming to Zurich for it would be assured of a seat – free, of course, as all admittance should be. In addition I would invite the local young people, universities, choirs etc. to attend. When everything is ready, I shall give three performances of *Siegfried* in a week. After the third performance the theatre will be pulled down and my score burnt! To the people who enjoyed it I shall then say, "Now go away and do it yourself!"'

Allowing for the pipe-dream quality of this letter, admitted by Wagner himself, we can nevertheless recognise in it the first particularised vision of what was eventually to become Bayreuth. Above all, it brings in for the first time the idea of a special building. Obviously one should not read into the 'crude theatre of planks and beams' anything more than the thought that this would be the cheapest way of building it. But in fact, as we find in practically all later references to a festival theatre, Wagner continually stressed the provisional or temporary nature of the building he wanted to erect – though there was no further talk of destroying the score after performance!

Behind his insistence there certainly lay the hope that a temporary theatre would relieve him of the attentions of philistine court theatre directors, who would scarcely be interested in anything so ephemeral. But there may, even at this stage, have been artistic considerations involved as well. Wagner was aware that his projected new work, *Siegfrieds Tod*, the text of which had been completed before he left Dresden, would present problems of staging. Many of his friends had openly told him so. Only Franz Liszt, who, after producing *Tannhäuser* in Weimar in 1849, went on the following year to give the first performance of *Lohengrin*, had sufficient faith in Wagner's genius to support him unquestioningly, and it was Liszt to whom Wagner in gratitude promised *Siegfrieds Tod*. However, in his autobiographical essay 'A Communication to my Friends' ('*Eine Mitteilung an meine Freunde*'), written a few months after his arrival in Switzerland, he admitted a change of mind: 'If I have since felt compelled to revise my plans very radically, so that it is no longer possible to carry them out in the form already notified to the public, the reason for this lies primarily in the nature of the poetic material.'

'Primarily' suggests that Wagner had other reasons beside purely dramatic ones for turning *Siegfrieds Tod* into *Der Ring des Nibelungen*, and it is not too rash to assume that among them might have been the feeling that the best way of ensuring a new start would be to write a work which by its very nature demanded the creation of new conditions to present it. This is in fact clearly enough implied in the 'Communication', in which he did not mention the building of a special theatre, though he did in a footnote provide another important indication of the radical change that had taken place in his approach to his work. The footnote reads: 'I am no longer writing *operas*: but, since I do not wish to invent some arbitrary name for my works, I call them simply *dramas*. This does at least describe most clearly the standpoint from which what I now have to offer should be regarded.' From all of this it seems a reasonable conclusion that Wagner's dogged insistence on a 'temporary' theatre owed something to his feeling that, until his vast new work was completed, he himself could not really know what the right conditions for its presentation would be.

The 'Communication' was already written and the decision

to expand the original Siegfried drama into a cycle of four works proclaimed when Wagner wrote once more to Uhlig (12 November 1851): 'The next revolution must necessarily put an end to our whole theatrical structure as it now exists. The theatres must and will all of them collapse – there is no way around that. From the ruins I shall gather together what I need – and I shall find what I want. I shall then erect a theatre on the banks of the Rhine and issue invitations to a great drama festival. After a year's preparation I shall present my complete work over four days: with it I shall reveal to the people of the revolution the meaning of this revolution in its noblest sense. The public will understand me; the present public cannot. Wild as this plan is, it is the only one on which I can stake my life, my work and my endeavour. If I live to see it, I shall have lived splendidly; if not, then I shall have died in a good cause.'

Only a few months later he was writing to another revolutionary friend in Dresden, August Röckel, of the possibility of putting his wild plan into effect in Zurich. The preparation for it would be a series of productions of his earlier works in the existing theatre, and in April 1852 he made a start with *Der Fliegende Holländer*. In July of the following year Liszt came to visit him in Zurich, and Wagner wrote afterwards to one of his new friends in Switzerland, Otto Wesendonck (13 July 1853): 'To my gratified surprise Liszt agreed with my plans for a festival, and we have decided that it shall be held in Zurich between the spring and autumn of some particular year. A temporary theatre will be built, and everything I need in the way of singers etc. will be specially engaged. Liszt will go to all corners of the earth to collect funds, and he is confident of raising the necessary money.'

It appears from this that what happened eventually in Bayreuth could have happened in Zurich some twenty years earlier. Why did it not come about? The immediate reason was undoubtedly the scepticism of the Swiss who, however honoured by Wagner's presence among them, were not prepared to pay out money for so bold and unpredictable a plan. But there was certainly a more personal reason involved: consciously or subconsciously, Wagner did not wish his theatre for the *Ring* to be built outside Germany. His work, still uncomposed, was not only revolutionary, but also demonstratively German. How could he, believing as he did in the moral influence of art, have hoped to further his cherished cause of a united Germany by building his stronghold in neutral Switzerland?

Confidently as he may have talked to Liszt and to his friends in Dresden about plans for producing the *Ring*, Wagner had not yet in fact solved the artistic problems posed by the work itself. That was yet another reason for regarding the building of a theatre for it in Zurich as premature. The first years of his Swiss exile were musically unproductive. Instead of writing operas, he sat down to work out his artistic ideas in words: during this period he wrote (among many other things) his long essays 'Art and Revolution', 'The Artwork of the Future' (*'Das Kunstwerk der Zukunft'*) and his full-length book *Opera and Drama*. The gap between theory and practice, as they affected the work of art itself, remained wide until that evening in September 1853 when he heard the E flat major chord of the *Rheingold* prelude in his mind's ear and at last unleashed his musical inspiration.

The composition sketch of *Das Rheingold* was already completed when, in February 1854, he wrote to Wilhelm Fischer in Dresden: 'In summer I shall start on *Die Walküre*; in spring 1855 it will be the turn of young Siegfried, and in the winter I hope to get down to Siegfried's death, so that everything will be ready by Easter 1856. Then I shall set about the impossible: procuring a theatre of my own, in which I shall produce my work before the whole of Europe as a great musical drama festival.' As usual, Wagner fell behind his programme. In 1855 he was in London, conducting a series of concerts for a living, *Die Walküre* still uncompleted.

London, however, proved profitable in another way. There he met a former close friend from Dresden, the architect Gottfried Semper who, also exiled for his part in the revolution, had settled in London. Here, clearly, was a useful ally in putting his plans for a festival theatre into effect. On his return to Zurich Wagner lost no time in persuading the Swiss authorities to offer Semper a post at the newly-opened polytechnic there. Semper accepted, and in the next three years Wagner and his architect friend were close neighbours.

Semper was no ordinary architect, but a man passionately devoted to the theatre. The opera house in Dresden in which Wagner brought out *Rienzi*, *Der Fliegende Holländer* and *Tannhäuser* was his creation. It could have been men such as he whom Wagner had in mind when, in a letter to Liszt in 1851 about a projected Goethe Foundation theatre in Weimar, he described an architect as 'the poet of the plastic arts, with whom sculptors and painters should stand in the same relationship as musicians and actors with the genuine poet.'

Whatever discussions Wagner and Semper may have had during those three years in Zurich concerning an actual theatre building, they could have been no more than theoretical. Wagner's growing feeling that his preoccupation with the *Ring* was causing him to lose touch with the world about him persuaded him to abandon it in the middle of *Siegfried* and to embark on a new work which would be less problematical and therefore simpler to stage.

This work was *Tristan und Isolde*. Wagner described his state of mind at this point of his life in his essay 'Report on the Fates and Circumstances that Attended the Execution of the Stage Festival Play Der Ring des Nibelungen' ('*Epilogischer Bericht über die Umstände und Schicksale, welche die Ausführung des Bühnenfestspieles* Der Ring des Nibelungen *begleiteten*'), written in 1871 to follow the *Ring* text in the sixth volume of his collected writings: 'For eight years no performance of any of my dramatic works had exercised a refreshing effect on my inventive powers of imagination; it had cost me endless trouble even occasionally to hear the sound of an orchestra. Germany, a country which was giving performances of my *Lohengrin* – a work I myself had not yet heard – remained closed to me. None of my German friends seemed to have any idea of the state of mind such deprivations induced in me . . . [They] tended rather to take the practical view that, by isolating myself for so long from association with the living theatre, I was in the process of sacrificing my former advantages, relapsing into the unpractical, unstageable and unsingable, and thus depriving my new works of any deserving claim to be performed. This fear turned, among all those who felt themselves thus exonerated from concerning themselves any further with me, to the comforting assumption that I was no longer a person to be reckoned with, and that was an appealing thought for those who had felt obliged to take account in their own activities of the expectations aroused by my earlier works. Our most famous opera reviewers regarded me as no longer among the living.

'Unfortunately it seemed as if some of those who had previously felt impelled to give their support to my great plan were not entirely unwilling to fall in with the ever-growing general view and to adopt an attitude of cautious reserve, and indeed, whenever I laid these silent scores one after another on my desk, I myself felt no urge to reopen them. I came at times to see myself as a sleepwalker, completely unconscious of what he was doing. When I raised my eyes from these scores to gaze at the bright daylight surrounding me, the awful daylight of German opera with its musical directors, its tenors, its sopranos and its programme anxieties, I could not help laughing aloud at the thought of the "silly rubbish" I was then trying to work on!'

The next few years can be seen as a renewed effort, born of frustration and despair, to come to some sort of terms with the existing theatre – still very much alive in spite of all the revolutions. But *Tristan und Isolde*, the revised *Tannhäuser* in Paris and finally *Die Meistersinger*, which refused in composition to conform to the modest proportions he had designed for it, must eventually have convinced Wagner that he had now finally passed the stage where compromise, even when he was resigned to it, was practically possible.

The two completed parts of the *Ring* cycle – *Das Rheingold* and *Die Walküre* – were also works with which Wagner could have attempted, even before *Tristan und Isolde*, to prove to his contemporaries that he was still an opera composer to be reckoned with. In 1861 an invitation did in fact come to him from Prague to produce and conduct *Das Rheingold* there. He turned it down. With the *Ring* there were to be no compromises: it was to be all or nothing. And he decided to make an attempt to win support for a special production by publishing the text of the *Ring* in full: it appeared in 1863.

There were two possibilities, he wrote in the foreword, to secure its production in the way he wanted: either with the help of a group of well-to-do, art-loving men and women or under the patronage of a German prince. He had little hope of the first, but could the prince be found?

As history knows, he was found. Wagner's book came into the hands of the young Crown Prince of Bavaria, whose first act, when he became King Ludwig II two years later, was to

summon Wagner to Munich and offer him unlimited freedom
to put his ideas into practice. Their partnership started out
auspiciously enough. Within a few months of their first
meeting Ludwig wrote to the composer: 'I have decided to
have a large stone theatre built, so that the production of *Der
Ring des Nibelungen* can be a complete one; this immortal work
must be given a framework worthy of its presentation.'

Wagner at once sent for Semper, who came to Munich to
show the king the plans which Wagner and he had already
worked out. The projected theatre's main features – the
amphitheatrical auditorium and the concealed orchestra –
were already familiar to Ludwig from Wagner's foreword
to the *Ring* poem, and the decision to build an interior
on these lines as a temporary structure inside an existing
exhibition building in Munich, and later to transfer it *en
bloc* to a grandiose permanent outer shell on the banks of the
river Isar, was one with which Wagner was for the moment
content. It would give him a chance to try out his ideas in
practice before committing himself to them finally, and it
would enable him to present his *Ring* cycle to his eager patron
without delay. In the timetable he drew up for the king in
those early, intoxicating Munich days the first performance
was scheduled for 1867–68.

There were certainly also other, unspoken reasons why
Wagner preferred a temporary to a permanent theatre in
Munich. The first lay in the nature of his dream – that
romantic dream, nursed for so many years, of some hastily erected wooden structure which would be pulled down
as soon as the performance was over. There was still in
Wagner's mind, when he wrote his foreword to the *Ring* in
1862, the idea of its production as a grand solitary gesture:
subconsciously perhaps he wanted Brünnhilde's liberating
act at the end of *Götterdämmerung* to wipe out the old order

entirely – including the very place at which it was performed. However, if this idea is too fanciful, one can certainly assume that Wagner had not entirely forgotten one of the basic conditions for his theatre: that it should be erected in one of the less large towns in Germany, so that visitors could approach the performance in a proper receptive spirit, unburdened by daily cares and undistracted by rival entertainments. Munich by its very size could not fulfil this condition, and the grudging spirit of its inhabitants, which rose to a positive fury when the news got about that Ludwig was proposing to build not only a festival theatre but a wide road and bridge leading to it as well, could not have failed to remind Wagner that this was not the theatre of which he had dreamed.

He continued, however, to support Ludwig's plans, even after his own indiscretions and the jealousies of the Munich court circles had forced him once again to take refuge in Switzerland. In order to give the king an impression of the proposed theatre, he asked Semper to make a model of it, and after viewing this in Zurich he wrote to Ludwig on 2 January 1867: 'It is a miracle: my idea, my suggestions and stipulations have been completely grasped by Semper's genius and carried out in so novel and practical a way that the noble simplicity of this conception must meet with the admiration of every connoisseur.'

A letter from Semper to Wagner, dated 26 November 1865, shows the nature of their collaboration: 'In the next few days you will receive from me a set of sketches on which I particularly want your opinion. I need to know whether its specifications match your intentions and ideas entirely . . . I should add that the present plan for the temporary festival theatre differs from the previous plan mainly in the fact that the central point of the concentric seating has been shifted in order to avoid from all angles a view into the orchestra. Then, in line with our discussions, I have put in two prosceniums, one behind the other, divided by the sunken orchestra. The narrower second proscenium is a smaller replica of the large one in front. This produces a change of scale and in consequence an apparent enlargement of everything on the stage, as well as the desired separation of the imaginary stage world from the real world on the other side of the intervening orchestra . . . This last is completely invisible, though the pit is not sunk all that low . . . I have not made the stage deep, as you can see, though with no intention of tying you and the stage mechanic (and/or scene designer) down in advance. On the contrary, I consider it most important to have your and the mechanic's view on this very point: whether the proposed depth is sufficient . . .'

This letter leaves no doubt at all that in the design of the festival theatre Semper saw his role as that of simply turning Wagner's ideas into practical architectural terms.

Only a few weeks after his letter to Ludwig in January 1867 praising the model of his theatre, Wagner wrote rather petulantly to Semper: 'If I were to think only of my own peace and security, I should feel bound to advise the king against building the theatre now, for everything to do with it that can be presented in an odious light will – as I do not need to tell you – be placed entirely to my account, while the whole credit will go to you.' However, he consented to continue supporting the plan, 'although my personal interest would not now urge me in that direction: in order to do justice to my artistic intentions I must concern myself with my creative preparations, which for the moment are still far removed from monumental buildings.'

In this letter one can see the resistance that was beginning to build up in Wagner's mind against the whole Munich project. Semper himself recognised it, as his reply of 4 February 1867 shows: 'For me creation is a joy in itself, the aim of my life, which can in any case last only a few more years. The putting off of this project to a later date would therefore mean my withdrawal from it – though incidentally I may say that I have always regarded my part as a secondary one, leaving you all credit for the ideas and inventions . . . If, as usual, it does not get beyond the planning stage, I shall have to comfort myself with . . . the thought that these preparatory sketches may prove useful to others when the work is taken up again – at least to provide a standard of comparison for even better things.'

Semper's forecast proved correct. Ludwig told Wagner in October 1867 of his decision to put off construction of the Munich theatre on financial grounds, and Wagner received the news without protest. Semper himself, denied by ministerial prevarication the promised consolation of a professorship at the Munich polytechnic, made himself unpopular both with the king and Wagner by insisting on full payment for the work he had put in on the sketches and models. He received his fee in the end, but at the cost of Wagner's friendship.

The idea of a festival theatre in Munich was now effectively dead, and perhaps for that very reason one can detect an improvement in the relations between Wagner and the king, rising to its climax at the first performance of *Die Meistersinger* in Munich the following year. What happened shortly after was, however, to flaw their friendship for ever: the king insisted on an immediate production of *Das Rheingold* and *Die Walküre* in the court opera-house.

Wagner's first reaction to the proposal was mild – not surprisingly, since he had himself, on 5 February 1868, suggested to the king's secretary that, once the stage of the court opera had been enlarged as planned, it would not be impossible, if Ludwig so wished, to produce the *Ring* parts there singly in succession. He told the king, however, that he could not undertake the production of *Das Rheingold* himself, but that he would, from his Swiss home, supervise its staging by persons of his own choosing. In a later letter (22 March 1869) he pointed out to Ludwig, 'This production will certainly differ in many ways from what you have so long intended. All the same, it should be possible in important points to demonstrate and justify its exceptional character.' Above all, it should not be more than a special private occasion, with guests admitted free on the king's direct invitation.

When it became clear that the king had no such intentions, and when Wagner heard of the difficulties his chosen henchmen were experiencing at the hands of the court theatre staff, his tone became more peremptory, and he attempted finally to stop or at least postpone the performance. This in turn roused Ludwig's fury – to an extent that would have shocked even Wagner if he had seen some of the private memoranda which the king was addressing to his secretary Düfflipp. 'The behaviour of Wagner and the theatre rabble can only be described as criminal and brazen. If Wagner's disgusting intrigues are allowed to succeed, the whole pack will become more and more impudent and shameless and will in the end be impossible to control . . . I have never heard of such insolence,' etc.

Though not directly addressed in such terms, Wagner could read between the lines and recognise that in the final analysis Ludwig was no different from all the other princes with whom he had had to do during his life: the royal whim was paramount. That calamitous production of *Das Rheingold*, followed in the ensuing year by a no more satisfactory one (from Wagner's point of view) of *Die Walküre*, convinced the composer that he had been right all along: the *Ring* did by its very nature demand the special production he had always dreamed of. The prince had failed him: he must now place his hopes in the other category of sponsors mentioned in his foreword to the *Ring* – the group of well-to-do, art-loving men and women.

It is possible that Wagner would not have explored this possibility, which he himself had dismissed in his foreword as hopeless, had it not been for another person whose importance to him waxed as Ludwig's waned. Indeed, there was some connection between the two events, for Ludwig's disillusionment with Wagner began when he realised how deliberately he had been deceived concerning the intimate relationship that had developed under his very nose between Wagner and Cosima, the wife of his conductor Hans von Bülow.

Without Cosima, said Nietzsche – who was a close friend of the Wagner household in Lucerne – Bayreuth would not have been possible. It is a judgement one can accept, and not only because she had more resilience and courage than Ludwig: her idealism and her belief in Wagner and his work were also far more practical. In addition to all that, she had supplied a new incentive by presenting him with children of his own. Fatherhood, coming to Wagner late in life, was an event of profound significance to him. A family man by nature, devoted to his mother, his brothers and his sisters, he had alleviated the frustrations of his childless marriage to Minna by taking a whole series of young musicians (as well as a young king) under his wing. Now these surrogate children had been replaced by real ones of his own. When, after two daughters, Cosima bore him a son in 1869, his pride and joy assumed almost absurd proportions. He informed his friend Pusinelli in Dresden, 'A fine strong son with high forehead and clear eyes, Siegfried Richard, will inherit his father's name and keep his works alive.' Without the rejuvenating effect of this primary fulfilment and without the driving force of his young second wife, who can say for certain whether Wagner would have found the strength and will to pursue his dream to the end?

When he first thought of Bayreuth as the place to launch his *Ring* tetralogy, Wagner did not in fact contemplate building a special theatre for it, but envisaged making use of the existing theatre there, the Markgräfliches Opernhaus, which reputedly possessed the largest stage in Germany. Certainly on paper Bayreuth fulfilled the conditions he had himself laid down for the site of his festival theatre: a small town, centrally situated in Germany and offering no rival distractions. It was also in the realms of his royal patron – an important consideration since, however much their friendship might have cooled, their mutual indebtedness remained. Besides, Ludwig was the legal owner of all rights in the *Ring* and he could, if he had a mind to, prevent a production of it even by the composer himself.

A single glance at the Markgräfliches Opernhaus, when he inspected it in April 1871, was enough to convince Wagner that this elaborate rococo building, erected a century earlier by Frederick the Great's sister, the Margravine of Bayreuth, could never provide a setting for the *Ring*. 'So we shall have to build – all the better,' wrote Cosima in her diary. Within a fortnight of his visit Wagner was writing to Ludwig's secretary, asking him to send on Semper's plans for the Munich theatre. He would, he assured Düfflipp, use in Bayreuth only such parts of it as were based on his own ideas.

The decision to build in Bayreuth was made before it was known where the money was to come from, though the proposed method of raising funds had been defined by Wagner in a 'Communication and Appeal to the Friends of my Art' ('*Mitteilung und Aufforderung an die Freunde meiner Kunst*'), written even before his visit to the town. It was a straightforward invitation to supporters to band together to provide funds. The details were worked out in more practical form in Berlin, the whole operation being placed in the hands of Countess Marie von Schleinitz, one of Wagner's powerful admirers, and the pianist Karl Tausig. Certificates of patronage (*Patronatscheine*) would be offered for sale to well-to-do persons, entitling their holders to seats at each performance. This would constitute the only means of admittance.

Here we see Wagner still sticking adamantly to his conviction, expressed as early as 1849 (in 'Art and Revolution'), that, the theatre being in the nature of a social necessity, entry to it must be free. Making admittance dependent on the advance purchase of an expensive certificate has, however, little to do with socialistic principles, particularly since this system would confine participation to a moneyed minority and such of their friends with whom they were willing to share their tickets. It was an essentially paternalistic system, and the credit for bringing Wagner back more into line with his early socialism must be given to Emil Heckel, a Mannheim bookseller who suggested the foundation of so-called Wagner societies (*Wagnervereine*) throughout Germany, which could buy certificates for sharing between their members drawn from less opulent circles.

On 22 May 1872, his fifty-ninth birthday, Wagner laid the foundation stone of his festival theatre in Bayreuth and made a long speech to his assembled supporters. When they next met, he told them, they would find on this spot a building in which they would be able to read the history of the thought that lay behind it. 'You will find, constructed with the cheapest of materials, an outer shell which will at best remind you of those sketchily built festival halls erected on odd occasions in German towns for singing and similar social events, to be immediately dismantled when the festival was over. On the other hand, you will on entering the building soon begin to see which of its aspects have been designed for permanence. Here too you will find very cheap materials, a complete lack of decoration; you will perhaps be surprised by the lack of ornament with which those traditional festival halls were pleasingly hung. But in the proportions of the interior and in its seating arrangements you will find the expression of an idea which, once grasped, will transform your expectations into something quite different from what you have ever before experienced in visiting a theatre. If this effect is fully achieved, the mysterious entry of the music will now begin to prepare you for the unveiling and display of scenic pictures which, by appearing to emanate from an idealistic dream world, should demonstrate to you the complete reality of the simulating powers of a noble art. Here nothing must be permitted to speak in mere provisional, sketchy forms; in scenery and in acting you will be offered the best that the artistic skill of our times can achieve.'

The things in which he placed his trust, Wagner went on, were the German national spirit, the spirit of German music, which awaited only the master's touch to rouse it, and the talent of the actors and singers who, as he knew from experience, could in the right hands be brought to an eager acceptance of the seriousness of their calling. Perhaps in times to come others would begin to believe in the things he believed in, and a splendid national theatre would be built somewhere in Germany. In the meantime, all he could do was to set the example with his own work.

One may doubt whether Wagner's reference to a national theatre, with its implication that this would provide a home for works other than his own, was in fact more than a piece of tactical window-dressing. In any case, as in his speech he tacitly admitted, what had started out in the youthful composer's mind as an attempt to reform the German theatre generally had been channelled by events into a desire to provide an ideal setting for the production of a single work, the *Ring* tetralogy. Can one believe, for example, that when Wagner referred in his speech to 'the mysterious entry of the music', he was thinking of anything except the low E flat of *Das Rheingold*? And how unerringly he gauged in advance the effect of that is evident to anyone who has ever heard it in his festival theatre at Bayreuth.

The erection of the theatre, under the supervision of the architect Otto Brückwald and the stage machinist Karl Brandt, is a story in itself that has been told many times and does not need to be repeated here. The most detailed account can be found in Cosima Wagner's diaries, which record in daily entries the unending series of negotiations regarding finance, administration and building technicalities, the copious correspondence with scene and costume designers, as well as the lengthy tours throughout Germany in search of suitable singers. It can be regarded as little short of a miracle that, beside all this, Wagner found time to complete the composition and orchestration of *Götterdämmerung*. The last note was written on 21 November 1874, ahead in fact of the completion of the festival theatre: full preliminary rehearsals of the whole *Ring* were already in progress when the final brick was laid on 1 August 1875.

The first festival took place in the summer of 1876, when three complete performances of the *Ring*, produced by Wagner himself, were given in the presence of a distinguished gathering of supporters and even crowned heads, including Emperor Wilhelm I of Germany, whose first words of greeting to Wagner were, 'I never believed you would be able to do it, but now the sun is shining on your work.' The verdict of King Ludwig, whose financial support at the eleventh hour had saved the festival from collapse before it was even launched, was predictably more concerned with the work than with the festival and its building: 'I feel born anew after experiencing those blissful days,' he wrote after attending the dress rehearsals. 'I am *burning* for the third performance, which will transport me out of this world and raise me, happy man, to the heights of ecstatic bliss!' He returned to Bayreuth for this, the final cycle.

To Wagner himself, unhappily conscious of the inevitable gap between the performance of his imagination and the performance he actually achieved, such praise brought little comfort. He wrote to Ludwig on 11 September 1876: 'The indisputable outward success of the festival, even the praise of many enthusiastic friends, cannot conceal from me the truth from which the last veil has now been torn: I know now that I and my work have no place in these times of ours . . . So it is now only for myself – and for you, my noble friend – that I shall strive to save my work. I shall continue to polish it until – as far as our badly managed and badly applied artistic means allow – it is brought to a state which is clear and understandable and at any rate correct, before handing it over to our fine fellow beings to be savaged. To start with, I intend to stage three more performances next summer: for these I shall try to achieve a better casting of some of the roles and, by giving it careful thought, to improve all the recognised deficiencies and incongruities of the production; the stage decorations also stand in need of considerable retouching and, at some points indeed, replacement. The means for this will come easily enough, since it will be possible this time to reduce the admission charges significantly, and the demand from all kinds of countries, now it is realised that there is every assurance of a great success, will presumably be very large, enabling me to devote the greater part of the proceeds to the payment of my artists. In the meantime, therefore – precisely because I cannot yet consider it to have been well enough presented – I shall hold my work back from any wider distribution.'

This letter gives a clear hint of what Wagner was thinking of when he made his cryptic remark, 'Next year we shall do it all differently,' to his choreographer Richard Fricke after the conclusion of the first festival. Though one can read into that utterance a doubt whether the style of production he had chosen was the right one, the slightly later letter to King Ludwig suggests that he still retained his faith in it, his dissatisfaction being due solely to the inadequacies of the execution. However, whatever his future intentions, the debts in which the first festival landed him made it impossible for him, in the six remaining summers of his life, to make another attempt at staging the *Ring*. It would have been a dismal ending to his dream of reforming German opera – if the existence of his festival theatre had not supplied a major incentive to the composition of his final work, *Parsifal*.

That work will be examined in detail in a subsequent chapter, and the only point that need be made here in regard to it is that, in his staging in the festival theatre in the summer of 1882, and in his insistence that the work should be performed nowhere else, Wagner reiterated in unmistakable terms his belief in the theatre as a place of divine revelation. That, once the copyright had expired, *Parsifal* joined the rest of his works to be 'savaged' in traditional opera houses throughout the world, might look at first sight like a final defeat of all Wagner's plans of theatrical reform. However, it is not to his productions alone that we should look in judging the success or failure of his ideas, nor solely to the philosophic theorising behind his attempt. In his foreword to the book containing the text of the *Ring*, published in 1863, he set out in plain practical language his reasons for building a theatre of his own. Here are some extracts from it:

'What no single theatre can offer can, with the help of good fortune, be achieved only by a combination of scattered forces, called together for a certain period of time at a definite location. The first advantage for the artists concerned would be that within this period of time they would need to give their attention to just one single task, the particular nature of which they would come to understand all the more swiftly and clearly in that their studies would not be interrupted by the distractions of their normal operatic routine. The positive result of this concentration of their intellectual resources on a single style and a single task cannot be overestimated, when one considers how little success could be expected from similar studies under normal conditions – when, for example, the same singer who sang on the previous evening in some badly translated recent Italian opera is called on to rehearse Wotan or Siegfried on the following day. In addition, this method would have the practical advantage that rehearsals would take up relatively much less time than would be possible within the context of normal repertory activities, and this in turn would add considerably to the fluidity of the rehearsal process . . .'

Stressing the vital importance of the amphitheatrical shape of the auditorium that enabled the orchestra to be hidden from sight, Wagner wrote: 'This will be clear to everybody who, wishing to gain a true impression of a dramatic interpretation, attends our usual opera performances and, through the unavoidable sight of the mechanical playing devices of instrumentalists and conductor, becomes the involuntary witness of technical evolutions which ought throughout to be concealed from him almost as carefully as the ropes and wires, the battens and boards of the stage decorations that, viewed from the wings, notoriously destroy all illusion. If, in addition, one has ever listened to the pure, ethereal tone of an orchestra heard through an acoustical sound barrier, freed of all the unavoidable non-musical sounds an instrumentalist makes in producing his notes, and if one imagines how advantageously the singer must appear to the onlooker when the space between them is uninterrupted, then one has only to add the ease with which the words can be understood to be persuaded of the success of my proposed acoustic and architectonic arrangements . . .

'Just as important as the performance itself will, in my opinion, be the effect of such a performance on the audience. Up till now accustomed, as a member of the opera-going public in a town, to seek thoughtless distraction in the very dubious performances of this ambiguous art form, and rejecting what this service has to offer as failing to provide what he is looking for, the visitor to our festival performances would suddenly find himself placed in an entirely different relationship to what is on offer. Clearly and definitively informed of what they can expect at this time and in this place, our audiences would consist of invited members of the public from far and wide, who would journey to the hospitable place of performance and meet there to absorb the impression of our performance. This visit at the height of summer might rightly be regarded by each individual as a refreshing excursion in which his first duty would be to shake off the cares of his daily round. Instead of having, in the usual way after a heavy and worrying day at the counter, in the office or laboratory or wherever his work may be, to seek relaxation and distraction in the evening – a state of mind for which mere superficial entertainment according to taste must seem the best remedy – he will now relax during the daytime and, with the onset of dusk, gather his wits together as the signal sounds for the start of the festival performance. Thus, his faculties refreshed and ready to be stirred, the first mysterious note from the hidden orchestra will arouse in him that contemplative mood without which no true artistic impression is ever possible. Impelled by his own yearning, he will follow eagerly, and will swiftly develop an understanding previously unknown, indeed inaccessible to him. Where his tired brain, in search of relaxation, had once encountered only tensions of another kind, leading to a painful overstretching of his faculties and in consequence grumbles about excessive length, excessive seriousness and even complete incomprehensibility, he will now have the invigorating experience of grasping things with an ease hitherto unknown to him. He will feel himself filled with a new warmth as within him a clear light is shed over things of which he had previously had no inkling . . .

'Though as a general rule I am not inclined to place too much reliance on the lasting effects of unwontedly stimulated emotions, I feel it can certainly be assumed [after this experience] that our players would find it impossible to relapse entirely into their former habits, and even more impossible after having seen their exceptional performances received in an equally exceptional way . . . All will have now seen and heard with their own eyes and ears what no mere exposition could ever have made clear to them; they will have absorbed directly the impression of a dramatic representation in which music and poetic action have combined, down to the smallest detail, to form a single whole. And they will have seen its effect on the audience as well as on themselves. It is impossible that this experience should fail to exert some influence on their own subsequent activities.'

No one who has experienced performances of Wagner's works at Bayreuth will be in any doubt of the correctness of his assumptions, and to these can be added the bonus of the acoustical qualities of the festival theatre itself, not yet in existence at the time that foreword was written, but eventually to become a monument as much to Wagner's practical skills as to his visionary powers. From this point of view the whole conception of Bayreuth can be regarded as itself a work of art as valid and enduring as the music dramas that directly and indirectly inspired it.

A Certain Something:
The Vision and Reality of Stagecraft

Wagner was as vitally concerned with the visual aspects of his dramas as with the words and music, and, if among his many talents he had possessed the ability to paint, he would surely have added scene painting to all the other activities he undertook in his theatre in Bayreuth. After dealing in 'The Artwork of the Future' with the architect's contribution to his ideal theatre, he described in somewhat ecstatic language the scene painter's role: 'The stage setting that is to convey to the audience the picture of human life must also, to ensure a full understanding of life, aim to represent a living picture of Nature, only within the bounds of which the artistic human being can come to see himself fully. The stage walls, which stare coldly and indifferently down on the actor and out to the audience, must adorn themselves with the fresh colours of Nature, with the warm light of the celestial ether, to be worthy of taking part in the human artwork. Plastic architecture here becomes aware of its limitations, its lack of freedom, and throws itself yearningly into the arms of pictorial art, there to discover its finest transformation into Nature.

'It is here that landscape painting makes its appearance, summoned by a common need that only it can fulfil. What the painter's happy eye extracts from Nature, what he as an artist seeks to reveal for the artistic enjoyment of the whole community, he will now add to the collective work

99

as his valuable contribution. Through him the stage setting attains its full artistic truth: his drawing, his colour, his warm, life-giving use of light force Nature to serve the highest of artistic purposes. What until now the landscape painter, in his urge to communicate what he has seen and grasped, has squeezed into the narrow frame of a picture, what he has hung on the lonely wall of an egoist's room or delivered up to an unconnected, irrelevant and distorting place in the serried rows of a picture store – with all this he will now fill the wide frame of the tragic stage, transforming the whole space into a living proof of his Nature-orientated creative power. What hitherto with his brush and his delicate mixture of colours he could only hint at he will now – through his artistic application of all available optical devices, of artistic lighting – raise to the level of a consummate illusory display.'

The most significant point in this lyrical outburst is Wagner's assertion of the necessity of depicting the human being as an integral part of Nature, and not as a self-contained species to which the natural world is merely incidental. In an earlier passage in the same essay he had identified as a shortcoming of ancient Greek art its conception of Nature as nothing more than 'a distant background' to humanity, under the command of gods who were themselves perceived in human form, and thus the error arose of regarding Nature as serving human ends rather than its own. Natural science and landscape painting, Wagner maintained, were the new developments that had enabled us to see Nature, artistically as well as scientifically, in its true light.

There is no work of his from *Der Fliegende Holländer* onwards in which this deeply-felt view of Nature as an independent force does not find direct dramatic expression in both words and music. It was therefore logical that, for its visual expression, he should feel the need of a scenic artist with the power to see more in his task than the mere provision of a few trees and hilltops for an exterior scene and a few doors and windows for an interior one. In his effort to attract only the best of artists for this work, Wagner suggested that 'the seeming grotesqueness of the methods employed in so-called scene painting', with its rough instruments and materials, would be fully compensated for by the end result, which in the context of a dramatic performance would stir hearts and minds in a way that no framed picture hung on the wall could hope to do.

The scenic directions contained in the text of his dramas can be seen, then, as first and foremost Wagner's descriptions for the painter's benefit of the kind of backgrounds he had in mind. This being the case, it is surprising to find in examining the scores how inconsistent the stage directions are in the amount of information they supply. Costumes, except in a few isolated instances, are not mentioned at all, and descriptions of the scenery range from virtually nothing to a detailed itemisation of every object in view on the stage. Here are a few examples of what confronted the artist Joseph Hoffmann when Wagner sent him the text of the *Ring* and invited him, after having read it thoroughly, to provide sketches for its scenery:

'An open space on a mountain height. The daybreak illuminates with increasing brightness a castle with gleaming battlements, which stands on a rocky summit in the background. Between this and the foreground of the stage a deep valley is to be imagined, through which the Rhine flows. Wotan and, beside him, Fricka, both asleep, are lying on a flowery bank at one side.' (*Das Rheingold*, Scene Two)★

★ This and the following stage directions from the *Ring* translated by Andrew Porter.

'In the middle stands a mighty ash-tree, whose prominent roots spread wide and lose themselves in the ground. The summit of the tree is cut off by a jointed roof, so pierced that the trunk and the boughs branching out on every side pass through it, through openings made exactly to fit. We assume that the top of the tree spreads out above the roof. Around the trunk of the ash, as central point, a room has been constructed. The walls are of rudely hewn wood, here and there hung with plaited and woven rugs. In the foreground, right, is a hearth, whose chimney goes up sideways to the roof; behind the hearth is an inner room, like a storeroom, reached by a few wooden steps. In front of it, half-drawn, is a plaited hanging. In the background, an entrance-door with a simple wooden latch. Left, the door to an inner chamber, similarly reached by steps. Further forward, on the same side, a table with a broad bench fastened to the wall behind it and wooden stools in front of it.' (*Die Walküre*, Act One)

'At the very back, the entrance to a cavern. The ground rises towards the centre of the stage, where it forms a small knoll; from there it descends to the cavern, so that only the upper part of the entrance is visible to the spectator. To the left, through the forest trees, a fissured cliff-face can be discerned.' (*Siegfried*, Act Two)

'The hall of the Gibichungs on the Rhine. This is quite open at the back. The background itself presents an open shore as far as the river; rocky heights border the shore.' (*Götterdämmerung*, Act One)

Wagner seems initially to have been very pleased with Hoffmann's sketches, even going so far in a letter to King Ludwig as to call his Valhalla for *Das Rheingold* 'a truly inspired stroke of genius'. But Cosima Wagner's diaries, while acknowledging the 'fine and powerful' impression they made, hinted at a looming dilemma: '. . . the only questionable aspect,' she wrote, 'being the downgrading of the dramatic intentions in favour of an elaboration of the scenery.' The sketches singled out for criticism from this point of view were that of Hunding's hut in *Die Walküre*, in which Hoffmann had faithfully followed Wagner's minutely detailed directions; and that of the hall of the Gibichungs in *Götterdämmerung*, for which Wagner had supplied virtually no directions at all. Hoffmann's design for the latter was judged to be too ostentatious, and Cosima recorded in her diary, 'R. is against all pomp,' his aim being 'to present human beings without conventional frills.'

The sketches clearly needed some simplification in order to make them suitable for stage use: Hoffmann's design for the second act of *Siegfried*, in which he showed the hero at the moment of confrontation with the dragon, sets the figures far in the background behind a veritable screen of trees. Finding the artist obdurate in defence of his sketches, Wagner turned them over to a pair of experienced scene painters, the brothers Max and Gotthold Brückner, for execution under Hoffmann's supervision. The arrangement led to a great deal of squabbling, which ended only with the removal of Hoffmann from active work on the scenery, consoled with the promise that he would still be credited as its original designer. It was an unfortunate start to Wagner's dream of a community of artists working happily together in a common cause.

There were difficulties too with the costume designer, Carl Emil Doepler. Wagner's first instructions to him likewise included an exhortation to read the text thoroughly before getting down to work, and he warned Doepler against the temptation to follow earlier artists in depicting the dress of Nordic figures in terms of classical antiquity. He might instead give his attention to 'passing references to the costumes of the Germanic peoples in Roman authors who came into contact with these nations,' but beyond that trust to his own inventiveness. That was a very necessary injunction, for costume is described in the stage directions, if at all, only in very vague terms – Sieglinde 'in a white garment', Siegfried 'in rough forest dress'. The single costume described in any detail is that of the Wanderer in *Siegfried*, who makes his first entrance 'wearing a long dark-blue cloak . . . On his head is a large hat with a broad, round brim, which hangs over his missing eye.'

Doepler's costume designs, Cosima wrote in her diary, 'really are very lovely, of great variety, and simple, suggesting to one a whole civilisation.' That might have been Wagner's opinion; Cosima herself did not fully share it, for she added, 'I myself should have preferred a more mystical impression, everything too clearly defined visually is to my mind detrimental to the effect of the music and the tragic action.' It was a perceptive comment, but one that, in the rush of getting the huge work on to the stage, failed to make its mark. The designs, with their ubiquitous winged helmets, their bejewelled armour, their pleated dresses and flamboyantly decorated shields, clearly pay little regard to Wagner's expressed desire to eschew pomp, and Cosima's famous final verdict on the eve of the first performance – that the costumes were 'reminiscent throughout of Red Indian chiefs' – seems all too well-founded.

The third important team member Wagner required for his staging of the *Ring* was a machinist, whose task it was to translate into stage terms all those stage directions that might be labelled visionary rather than purely practical. These are mainly descriptions of action and, unlike the background settings, they involve the use of machinery on an open stage as well as the participation of the actors. Wagner did not specifically consider the work of the machinist (later described in his retrospective essay on the production of *Parsifal* as 'scenic dramaturgy') in his theoretical writings. This is surprising, when one recalls that scenes dependent on machinery figure in almost all his works, if nowhere quite as abundantly as in the *Ring*, with its swimming Rhinemaidens, its rainbow bridge, its Valkyries riding horses through the sky, its fearsome dragons, and the fire and flood of the final cataclysm.

Did Wagner really expect these to be staged as he described them in his stage directions? The answer, on the evidence of his own production at Bayreuth, must be that he did, and he cannot on that account be suspected either of ignorance or of sublime indifference towards the practical limitations of the stage. On the contrary, he was an experienced man of the theatre who knew at first hand what the machinists of his day could produce in the way of spectacular effects. He may have despised the use of spectacle merely for its own sake – one of the besetting sins, in his eyes, of the operatic tradition he was striving to overcome – but that did not prevent him from using it himself to make a genuine dramatic effect, as in the first act of *Der Fliegende Holländer*, where his stage direction reads: 'The storm begins again to rage violently, and it grows darker. In the distance the Flying Dutchman's ship appears, with blood-red sails and black masts. It swiftly approaches the shore on the side opposite to the Norwegian ship and drops anchor with a fearful crash. Daland's steersman awakes with a start. Without leaving his place, he casts a hasty look at the rudder and, satisfied that no harm has been done, he hums the beginning of his song and falls asleep again. Silently, and in the complete absence of any other noise, the ghostly crew of the Dutchman furl the sails.'

This thrilling moment – the one we all wait for in any performance of *Der Fliegende Holländer* – was well within the capabilities of most of the existing theatres of the time, and Wagner had no qualms about entrusting it to their machinists' skill. An equally thrilling moment in *Tannhäuser* – the transition in the first act from the Venusberg to the valley below the Wartburg – is indicated in the text and score only by the brief stage direction: 'The scene changes with lightning speed.' In his guide for future producers of the work Wagner explained how this had been done in the first production:

'The scenery for the Venusberg, which in its construction must correspond exactly to the already fully prepared Wartburg valley scenery behind it (in which connection the hill projections, necessary in both scenes, are very convenient), is in its main points sufficiently indicated in the score. A difficulty remains, however, with the subsequent veiling of the scene behind rosy clouds, when this has to be done in a confined space: the intended magical effect would be destroyed if this were done by a clumsy lowering of a solid canvas flat depicting clouds. In Dresden, after painstaking rehearsal, the veiling was carried out very aptly and effectively by the gradual lowering of delicately painted gauzes, of which several were let down in succession. Only then, when the contours of the previous scene were no longer recognisable, was a solid canvas flat, painted pink, brought on behind the gauzes to close the scene off completely. Strict attention was paid to the tempo to ensure that it corresponded with the music. The scene change was then done at a single stroke when, during a sudden darkening of the stage, first the solid canvas flat and then in rapid succession the gauzes were pulled up, and light, immediately breaking through, suffused the new scene, the valley, with the clearest brightness of day. The effect of this valley scene, which must precisely reflect the directions in the score, should be so overpoweringly fresh, serene and heart-warming that poet and musician can safely allow the audience a considerable time to absorb it.'

Such assured stagecraft, as effective today as when it was first applied, is the strongest argument in favour of taking Wagner at his word when it comes to staging his works, certainly as regards the early ones, and the same can be said of *Die Meistersinger*. But the other works of his maturity do rouse certain doubts concerning the feasibility of applying such techniques to them. With the working out of his new conception of music drama based on myth, Wagner deliberately turned his back on historical reality. His object now was to portray his characters from within, and through his music to enable us to experience directly inside ourselves the agonies of their various dilemmas. In the earlier works we are still, as we would be in real life, on the outside looking in: we are detached observers, sympathetic or unsympathetic as our own judgement dictates, and as observers we need to be consciously aware of the outward circumstances amid which the drama is taking place. In the later works, in which we are no longer mere observers, but direct participants, the outward circumstances are important to us only to the extent that they are important to the characters whose emotions we are sharing.

It is a difference that demands an equally different approach to the matter of scenery. That Wagner was not blind to the problem can be shown by comparing the first act of *Der Fliegende Holländer* with the first act of *Tristan und Isolde*, both of them set against a background of ships and sea.

The stage direction for the arrival of the Dutchman's ship has already been quoted. It is full of movement, and in his remarks on its staging (in a short essay written just after his guide to the production of *Tannhäuser*) Wagner stressed even more strongly the importance of depicting the stormy seas and the ships as realistically as possible, enjoining producers to observe exactly the scenic instructions scattered throughout the score: 'The sea between the cliffs must appear as rough as it is possible to achieve: the nearer the manipulation of the ship to complete reality, the better. Small details, such as the rocking of [Daland's] boat when struck by a large wave (between the verses of the steersman's song), must be done very drastically.'

There is no call for movement of any kind in the very brief description of the setting for the first act of *Tristan und Isolde*: 'Tent-like room on the foredeck of an ocean-going ship, richly hung with tapestries. At the start these are closed, completely blocking out the background. Some narrow steps to one side lead down to the ship's hold.' The scene, when the tapestries are drawn back, is also virtually devoid of movement: 'The ship is seen lengthways back to the poop, and beyond it the sea and the horizon. Sailors are seated around the mainmast, occupied with ropes; beyond them on the poopdeck knights and squires are seen, also seated; at some distance from them Tristan stands with folded arms, gazing thoughtfully out to sea; at his feet, stretched out comfortably, lies Kurwenal.'

Though the sea is calm, as Isolde informs us, the ship is making steady progress towards its dreaded goal, and, if we are to be realistic, we must expect wind enough to sway the ship and stir the flimsy sides of Isolde's 'tent-like room'. However, we have no wish for realistic effects at this point, and neither, very clearly, had Wagner. His intensely introspective orchestral introduction has led us firmly into an emotional state in which any attempt at realism would be as disturbingly alien to the dramatic action as the absence of it would be in *Der Fliegende Holländer* after that work's stormy, windswept overture. The single hint of realistic action in the scene – the sight of the sailors 'occupied with ropes' – can easily be accepted as symbolic in Isolde's eyes of the cruelly unheeding outside world in which she is completely powerless. It is in any case a very brief glimpse, and it is more than likely that Wagner deliberately invented something simple and static for his crowd players to do in order to prevent them from thinking up more extravagant ways of drawing attention to themselves.

Tristan und Isolde was written with a traditional theatre in mind, and Wagner took care to make no scenic demands that would be regarded as impracticable. With the *Ring*, however, he was under no such constraint. The theatre in which it was to be staged had not yet been built, and, when he should eventually find the means to build it, he would be in a position to ensure that it would be designed to meet the demands of his work, not the other way round. And there was a further practical advantage: since the stage would be used exclusively for performances of the *Ring*, the machinists would have time and opportunity to carry out operations far more elaborate than they could normally hope to achieve. 'The scenery for my *Rheingold*, for instance,' he wrote in his introduction to the text of the *Ring*, published in 1863, years before his theatre was built, 'would be quite unthinkable in theatres like those in Germany with a daily changing repertoire, whereas, under the favourable conditions I have here described, scenic designers and machinists would be given all the opportunities they could possibly wish to demonstrate their art as the true art it really is.'

When he first embarked in 1848 on the work that was eventually to become the *Ring* tetralogy, Wagner was still thinking in terms of the traditional theatre, and *Siegfrieds Tod*, his first version of *Götterdämmerung*, ends, after Brünnhilde's leap into Siegfried's funeral pyre, with the reappearance of Alberich, who urges Hagen to recover the ring. The stage direction reads: 'Hagen turns swiftly and, preparing to jump into the flames, throws away his spear and his shield. Suddenly, from the fiery glow a blindingly bright light emerges: on a dark cloud (resembling the steam from an extinguished wood fire), the light rises upwards, and Brünnhilde, in helmet and shining armour, is seen within it as, on a gleaming horse, she leads Siegfried by the hand through the air. As the cloud floats upwards, the waves lapping the banks of the Rhine rise to the level of the hall; the three mermaids, borne on the waves and illumined by moonlight, carry off the ring and the magic helmet. Hagen rushes at them like a madman to snatch the ring from them; the mermaids seize him and drag him with them down into the depths. Alberich sinks to the ground with a despairing gesture. The curtain falls.'

This, though complicated enough, would certainly have been within the capabilities of the technicians of that time. However, what Karl Brandt, Wagner's machine director at Bayreuth, encountered at the same point in *Götterdämmerung* was this: 'The flames immediately blaze up so that they fill the whole space in front of the hall, and appear to seize on the building itself . . . When the whole space of the stage seems filled with fire, the glow suddenly subsides, and only a cloud of smoke remains; this drifts to the background and lies there on the horizon as a dark bank of cloud. At the same time the Rhine overflows its banks in a mighty flood which pours over the fire. On the waves the three Rhinemaidens swim forwards and now appear above the pyre. Hagen, intent on recovering the ring from Brünnhilde before the Rhinemaidens do, rushes like a madman into the flood, the Rhinemaidens seize him and carry him off. Through the cloudbank, which has settled on the horizon, a red glow breaks out with increasing brightness. By its light, the three Rhinemaidens are seen, swimming in circles, merrily playing with the ring on the calmer waters of the Rhine, which has gradually returned to its bed. From the ruins of the fallen hall, the men and women, in great agitation, watch the growing firelight in the heavens. When this reaches its greatest brightness, the hall of Walhall is seen, in which gods and heroes sit assembled . . . Bright flames seize on the hall of the gods. When the gods are entirely hidden, the curtain falls.'*

Acknowledged master of his profession as he was, even Brandt could find no sure way of coping successfully with this cataclysmic spectacle, and in his retrospective account of the 1876 festival Wagner was obliged to admit that the machinery had functioned properly in none of the performances. It was not the only scene in the *Ring* which presented difficulties in that first production and which has caused all producers and technicians difficulties ever since. To mention just one other, here is Wagner's stage direction for the fight between Siegfried and the giant Fafner, who has transformed himself into 'a huge, scaly dragon': 'He draws his sword, springs towards Fafner and stands in an attitude of defiance. Fafner drags himself further up the knoll and spits from his nostrils at Siegfried. Siegfried avoids the venom, leaps nearer, and stands to one side. Fafner tries to reach him with his tail. When Fafner has

* Translated by Andrew Porter

nearly caught Siegfried, the latter leaps with one bound over the dragon, and wounds him in the tail. Fafner roars, draws his tail back quickly, and rears up the front part of his body to throw its full weight on Siegfried, thus exposing his breast. Siegfried quickly notes the place of the heart and plunges his sword in there up to the hilt. Fafner rears up still higher in his pain, and sinks down on the wound, as Siegfried lets go of the sword and leaps to one side.'*

It seems unlikely that Wagner would have expected either the actor playing Siegfried or the machinists manipulating the dragon to carry out the movements exactly as he had described them, though we know from colleagues' accounts that he always tried to come as close to his stage directions as possible. In this case he evaded the issue by placing the fight at the very back of the deep Bayreuth stage. In making this decision, he may have been influenced to some extent by anxiety due to the failure of the dragon to arrive from London in time for thorough rehearsal, but he may also have come to the conclusion that this time he had demanded a little too much. As a producer he was not above ignoring his own printed stage directions when he felt he had miscalculated their effect: for instance, he banished the horse Grane from the lengthy scene in *Die Walküre* between Brünnhilde and Siegmund, in which, according to the text, it was to be present throughout. It was, he realised, too distracting.

We should have had a better idea of Wagner's own view of the inviolability or otherwise of his stage directions if he had written down the changes he made during his Bayreuth production for use in a later edition of the score. The fact that

* Translated by Andrew Porter

he did not suggests that he did not regard his production as decisive. 'Costumes, scenery, everything must be done anew for the repeat performances,' he told Cosima after the festival ended. Since there were no repeat performances at Bayreuth in his lifetime, there was no opportunity of providing what future generations could look on as a definitive text of the *Ring*.

With *Parsifal*, happily, the position is different, for the stage directions in the musical score, published after Wagner's Bayreuth production of 1882, diverge in a number of particulars from those in the original text, which was published before the staging took place. What is immediately apparent is that they are considerably more detailed than in any of the previous works. We find for the first time exact descriptions of costumes. The Knights of the Grail and their squires all wear robes 'similar to those of the Knights Templars: white tunics and mantles, with a hovering dove instead of a red cross displayed on their shields and mantles'; Kundry appears in the first act in 'rough clothing, long skirt hitched up, a belt of snake-skins hanging down low,' and in the second act in 'lightly draping, fantastic clothing, somewhat Arabian in style'. There is also for the first time some reference to physical appearance: Gurnemanz is described as 'robustly aged', Kundry in the first act as having 'a dark reddish-brown complexion and piercing black eyes, at times flashing wildly, more frequently fixed in a death-like stare'.

These, it should be pointed out, are the only descriptions of this sort: no indication is given of the clothing of Klingsor or indeed of Parsifal himself before his entry in black armour in the third act. Such directions, however inconsistent in their application, were clearly meant to stimulate – alternatively, following his experiences with the *Ring* production, to curb

– the imagination of costume designers and make-up artists at vital points in the drama. In his own production, which in any case he meant to be the only one, Wagner made doubly sure by exercising a tight control over his scenic designer, Paul von Joukowsky, and his costume designers, even to the extent of making rough sketches himself to show exactly what he wanted.

'It is no use to me when clever costume designers or landscape artists send me nice pretty sketches, suitable for something like artists' balls or court masquerades,' he wrote to King Ludwig on 17 May 1881. 'But so it goes with everything I do: everyone thinks he has better – and of course finer – ideas than I myself, when all I want is a certain something, a quite definite poetic effect, but on no account the usual operatic theatre spectacle. It is the same with scenery, which is always designed as if it were to stand entirely by itself, to be looked at rather like a panorama, just as the fancy takes, while what I want is just an unobtrusive practical background and setting for a characteristic dramatic situation.'

Wagner himself chose the cathedral at Siena as his model for the Temple of the Grail and a garden in Rapallo for Klingsor's realm in the second act, and all Joukowsky was required to do was to translate these into stage terms – a task which involved him in having to redraw his sketches sometimes as many as seven times before he could satisfy Wagner's wishes. The flower costumes for Klingsor's maidens, only vaguely described in the stage directions, proved particularly problematic, and the final result, as photographs show, bore little resemblance to Wagner's original conception, as expressed in his letter to King Ludwig, of a garment formed out of two flower cups. The costumes for the Knights of the Grail and their squires did not conform exactly to the pattern set down in the first published text. Whatever the reason for the change – possibly the on-stage effect of their being all dressed similarly proved too monotonous – Wagner found it so compelling that he suppressed his entire description of the knights' costumes in the musical score.

Other stage directions to undergo changes as a result of the production include the transformation scenes in the first and third acts. Transformation scenes are a constantly recurring feature of Wagner's works, and they stem from his feeling that the dramatic and musical flow of each act should never be interrupted by a lowering of the main curtain. To avoid this necessity, he used at various times all the traditional obscuring devices: lighting dissolves and blackouts, gauzes, steam and even (when all else failed) an inner curtain on stage (as in the third acts of *Lohengrin* and *Die Meistersinger*). In *Parsifal*, however, he attempted something new and much more complicated: the transition from one scene to another with actors still on stage.

In the first act the stage direction reads: 'Gradually, as Gurnemanz and Parsifal appear to be walking, the scene changes, from left to right, in an imperceptible manner; thus, the forest disappears, a door opens between the rock faces, which now enclose the two men; then they become visible again in upward-sloping passages, along which they appear to be walking. They arrive at last in a huge hall.' This was changed in the musical score into a direction that presumably describes the transformation as it was actually done, against a background of moving backcloths: 'Gradually, as Gurnemanz and Parsifal appear to be walking, the scene has already begun with increasing perceptibility to change; thus, the forest disappears, and an archway opens between the rock faces, which now enclose the two men.

The scene, moving through upward-rising passages, becomes completely transformed: Gurnemanz and Parsifal now enter the huge hall of the Temple of the Grail.'

Similar stage directions describe the transformation in the third act, now moving in the opposite direction.

At first glance the difference between the original versions and the amended ones may seem slight, but a closer look reveals two significant changes. Firstly, the actors, instead of remaining in sight throughout, are ushered off swiftly, to reappear only when the transformation is complete; and secondly, the transformation itself is no longer to be done 'in an imperceptible manner', but 'with increasing perceptibility'. These are clear concessions to practical realities.

Even in their modified form, the transformations caused great technical difficulties, and it was no doubt memories of similar frustrations with the *Ring*, together with the weariness of age, that forced Wagner uncharacteristically to yield to a suggestion from Emil Scaria (his Gurnemanz) that the visual representation of the third act transformation be omitted entirely. Cosima noted in her diary, after seeing the effect of this in rehearsal, 'We are pleased that the curtain now falls and no transformation scenery disturbs the music.'

Whether this 'we' included Wagner himself there is no way of discovering, and we can only speculate on the possessor of the unknown hand that struck out this sentence in Cosima's diary (20 July 1882). Could it have been Wagner himself? At any rate, we know that, though the curtain was closed in the third act throughout the first festival of 1882, the visual transformation was restored, the difficulties having been sorted out, in the following year, in accordance with Wagner's wishes as expressed in the stage direction of both original text and later musical score.

It is a source of constant argument whether Wagner's stage directions can be taken as a reliable guide to the manner in which he wished his works to be presented. My own opinion is that, though helpful in certain respects (and more so in *Die Meistersinger* and *Parsifal* than in the other works), they are of very limited practical value in shaping a complete production. The main guide to the valid representation of any dramatic work lies in the words and music themselves – a truth of which Wagner was very well aware, as his constant exhortations to everyone concerned in the production to make themselves thoroughly familiar with the text before starting work clearly show. That he felt it so necessary to stress this obvious fact again and again was a reflection of his conviction, based on experience, that all the people engaged in the opera houses of his day had completely forgotten it.

His decision to include stage directions in the texts of his dramas – by no means a usual practice at the time – may have originated in a desire to stimulate the imaginations of these hidebound people, compelling them to look at his drama as a whole, instead of giving their attention only to the part that directly concerned each one of them. This speculation would go at least some way towards accounting for the inconsistent provision of scenic descriptions, varying in detail according to the vividness of the pictures in his own mind at the time of writing.

The fact that, when he came to stage his works himself, he chose to carry out his stage directions as literally as possible should also be seen in an historical context. The Duke of Meiningen's theatre company that is generally recognised as the originator in Germany of stage realism, with its meticulous attention to historical accuracy in settings and costumes and its naturalistic handling of crowd scenes, made its first impact in 1874, only two years before the launching of the *Ring* in Bayreuth. Wagner, who in view of the dates can be absolved from a suspicion of imitating the Meiningen methods, certainly admired them, and he found an ally as well as a friend in the Duke of Meiningen himself, whose principal scene painters, incidentally, were also the brothers Brückner. Engaged, then, as he was in demonstrating in Bayreuth a thoroughly revolutionary new style of production, he can scarcely be reproached for having neglected to look beyond it to a time when that style of production would itself seem traditional and outmoded.

And, in any case, we should bear in mind that Wagner was far from satisfied with his own production efforts. The idealistic visions of the role of scenery outlined in 'The Artwork of the Future' (1849) had given way in the light of experience to the simple desire, expressed in his letter of 1881 to King Ludwig, for 'an unobtrusive practical background'. Yet there still remained that 'certain something' as the final goal, and the way towards it could perhaps only be defined in negatives. The Wagner who banished metronome markings from his scores, claiming that the correct tempo was implicit in the music and a sensitive conductor would find it for himself, wrote in a letter (25 January 1854) to his friend August Röckel, who had complained of a lack of clarity in parts of the *Ring* text, 'I believe that a true instinct has kept me from being too explicit, for I have come to feel that an absolute disclosure of the intention prevents genuine understanding.'

This remark was not directed specifically at scenery, but it would surely not be wrong to apply it to that too. The descriptions of Hunding's hut and Siegfried's fight with the dragon, for example, might be over-explicit, but these are the exceptions rather than the rule. The remaining stage directions – the vast majority, in fact – might better be regarded, not as instructions to be slavishly followed, but as stimulants to imagination and safeguards against a relapse into traditionalism in the unending, but often in itself rewarding search for that elusive 'certain something'.

The Art of Noble Deception:
The Role of the Actor–Singer

After describing in his essay 'The Artwork of the Future' the part to be played by architects and painters in the realisation of his ideal theatre, Wagner went on to discuss the role of the actor. These are his words: 'On the stage created by the architect and the painter there now enters the artistic human being, in the same way that the natural human being enters the showplace of Nature. What sculptors and historical painters have endeavoured to depict in stone and on canvas, these now bring to conscious artistic life in themselves, through their figures, their limbs, their facial features. The same sense that guided the sculptor in understanding and representing the human form now guides the *actor* in the treatment and deportment of his actual body. The same eye that enabled the historical painter to reveal in line and paint, through arrangements of clothing and compositions of groups, all that was beautiful, appealing and characteristic now commands the full range of actual human appearance. Sculptors and painters once freed Greek tragic actors from the cothurnus and the mask, upon which and behind which the real person could conduct himself only within the limits of a specific religious convention. Rightly, these two plastic arts did away with this final distortion of the pure, artistic human being, and in this way anticipated in stone and on canvas the tragic actor of the future. As they once revealed him in all his undisguised truth, now they must leave him to show himself in reality, to bring the figure they in some respects described to life in his own body.

'Thus will the illusion of the plastic arts become truth in drama: the plastic artist extends his hand to the *dancer*, to the *mime*, and is thus absorbed into him, becoming himself dancer and mime. The task of the latter will be to transmit the inner being, his feelings and desires, as far as lies within his power, to the eye. The scenic setting in all its width and depth lies open to him for a plastic demonstration of his form and movement, either as a single person or in combination with his fellow mimes. But where his capacity ends, where the full expression of his feelings and desires urges him to *speech*, then words will define his clearly perceived object: he will become a *poet*, and, in order to be a poet, a *composer*. Yet as dancer, composer and poet he is still one and the same person, nothing other than *a human actor-artist appealing with the utmost range of his capabilities to the utmost degree of susceptibility.*

'In the actor himself the three sister arts combine to produce a common effect in which the greatest potentiality of each is displayed to its fullest advantage. By operating together, each one gains the power to be and to achieve exactly what, according to its own particular nature, it strives to be and to achieve. Since each can, at the point where its own capacity ends, merge into the next (from then on more effective) art, each preserves its own purity, freedom and independence. The *dancing mime* rids himself of his incapacity as soon as he is allowed to sing and speak; *musical works* attain general comprehensibility through the mime as well as through the spoken word, precisely to the extent that the music is capable of merging into the movements of the mime and the words of the poet. But the *poet* becomes truly human only when he is transformed into the flesh and blood of the *actor*; if he subjects every artistic aspect to the aim that binds them all together and leads to a common goal, this aim can be turned from wish to reality only when the poetic wish is made subservient to the acting possibilities.'

This view of the actor's art in the drama as a whole, and the almost visionary terms in which it is expressed, may seem over-idealised, but it does in fact reflect a lifelong conviction on Wagner's part that found a more practical expression in his essay 'On Actors and Singers' (*'Über Schauspieler und Sänger'*), written in 1872, when he was actually engaged in the building of his ideal theatre in Bayreuth. Pointing out that, as experience has shown, a good performance can make a bad play appear better than it is, whereas a bad performance can ruin a good play, he commented: 'This, on a close view, must lead us to the conclusion that in theatre performances the true art can be attributed solely to the actors, whereas the author shares in this "art" only to the extent that in the shaping of his play he has paid heed first and foremost to the anticipated effect of its dramatic representation . . . When we look more closely at what is characteristic in the performance of an outstanding actor, we are amazed to see in it the basic elements of each and every art in all its diversity, expressed with a force no other art can attain. What the plastic artist copies from Nature the actor imitates indistinguishably to the life, thus exercising over the imagination of the onlooker a power in every way equal to that which, as if by magic, he exercises over himself, his outermost person as well as his innermost feeling.'

Later in the same essay Wagner repeated his almost humble definition of the dramatist's role in relation to the actor's. Following a discussion of the performing conventions of the ancient Greek theatre, he wrote: 'The work of the dramatist depended more almost on his contribution as choreographer and chorus leader than on his purely poetic power of story telling. Everything that the poet invents in that capacity and sets out in the minutest detail is an elucidation, as exact as possible, of the picture he saw at the moment of conception, and this he now holds up to the acting fraternity for imitation in an actual staged drama.'

The final sentence does in fact give the lie to the picture of the author, in both this and the earlier essay, as little more than the provider of vehicles for actors to display their talents. In his essay 'On Actors and Singers' Wagner was defending his own habit of writing into his scores instructions of how a particular passage should be played or sung, a practice denounced by some critics as depriving singers of their freedom of expression. He declared that singers themselves looked on these instructions 'with proper instinct' as no more than suggestions for them to build on. And it is true, as we know from singers' accounts of his work as a producer, that he did not insist on a precise manner of doing things, as long as he was satisfied that the singer understood what he was required to express and expressed it in an effective way.

Wagner's veneration for actors was genuine, but what he could not bear was the thoughtless routine into which so many of them – and particularly opera singers – had fallen, either through laziness, vanity, stupidity or the theatrical practices of his day, which encouraged superficiality. He attributed this to the influence of the Italian and French schools, which had contributed most to the development of opera, whereas the Germans had confined themselves to the modest *Singspiel*, which was more in the nature of a play that used music simply to provide colour or tension at certain high points in the action. The weakness of the Italian method was, in his view, that it emphasised the singing purely for its own sake, paying only perfunctory attention to the dramatic action; of the French, that it followed the artificial traditions of French spoken drama, in which the words were paramount and the action formalised. The *Singspiel*, though potentially offering a better balance than either, suffered in practice by being entrusted to straight actors, which meant that no great demands could be made on their singing talents, and this in turn ensured that the range of the drama itself remained restricted. It was not until composers of the calibre of Mozart (*Die Zauberflöte*), Beethoven (*Fidelio*) and Weber (*Der Freischütz*) adopted it that the *Singspiel* began to develop into a true operatic form, but initially it encountered two obstacles. Firstly, the specialised singers the music called for had for the most part no acting talent (or saw no need for it) and the dialogue passages were thus apt to become embarrassing; and secondly, these great composers, lacking a precedent, succumbed to the temptation of casting their solo and ensemble passages in the prevailing Italian style, while making no attempt to solve the problem of the spoken dialogue.

Believing as he did that the only truly German operatic form lay in the area of an 'extended' *Singspiel*, Wagner set himself to find a way of replacing the spoken dialogue with a musical setting more suited to the German language than the *secco recitativo* of the Italians or the fiery rhetoric of the French. He wrote in his essay 'On the Performing of *Tannhäuser*' ('*Über die Aufführung des* Tannhäuser', 1852): 'There is no distinction in my opera between so-called "declaimed" and "sung" phrases. My declamation is song, and my song declamation. The clearly defined cessation of "song" and the clearly defined entry of the otherwise customary "recitative", through which in opera the singer's delivery is usually divided into two quite separate modes, have no place in my works. I have absolutely nothing in common with the traditional Italian recitative, in which the composer hardly indicates the rhythm of the delivery at all, leaving it to the discretion of the singer. In those passages where the text sinks down from a lyrical surge of excited emotion to a simple statement of feeling I have never relinquished my right to indicate the mode of delivery just as clearly as in the lyrical passages. Consequently, whoever confuses these passages with recitatives of the usual kind, and changes or adapts the stipulated rhythm to suit his own fancy, disfigures my music just as much as he would by introducing different notes or harmonies into my lyrical melodies. Since in all these passages that look like recitative I have taken care to indicate, rhythmically as well as otherwise, exactly the expression I am aiming at, I therefore request all conductors and singers to begin by rehearsing them with strict adherence to the note values as written and in a tempo suited to the nature of the speech. If I find myself in the happy position of seeing the mode of delivery laid down by me correctly understood by the singers, and if this has been fully absorbed by them, I shall then urge them to an all but complete abandonment of a strict adherence to the musical beat, which up to this point has functioned merely as a mechanical aid to agreement between composer and singer: once full agreement has been achieved, it can be cast aside as a tool that, having served its purpose, is now as useless as it is burdensome. From now on the singer, having understood the effect I was aiming at and made it fully his own, may give free rein to his own natural feelings and even to the physical necessities of his breathing in moments of emotional excitement. The more self-creative he can become through having complete freedom of emotional expression, the more I shall be indebted to him. The conductor's task is then simply to follow the singer with the orchestral accompaniment intact.'

Then, in order to forestall any criticism that in the latter part of this injunction he was giving away all that he had claimed for the composer at the beginning, he added: 'I need hardly mention that the mode of delivery I have here outlined – the highest attainable in any kind of artistic interpretation – is not to be confused with the usual practice, which gives its blessing to the conductor who with sycophantic care puts his intelligence and practical skill solely to the task of following the caprices of our prima donnas. In the latter case he is the indispensable cover for outrageous improprieties, in the former he is a fellow creative artist.'

At the time of composing *Tannhäuser* Wagner had yet to acquire the skill which in the later works so reduced the difference between the recitative passages (the words necessary to move the action on) and the lyrical ones (the words with which the actors express their emotions) that singers were no longer misled into distinguishing between them in their style of delivery. He was, as he admitted in his later essay 'On Actors and Singers', himself partly to blame, through his inexperience both as composer and as producer, for the fact that *Tannhäuser* succeeded on the strength of its melodies rather than its dramatic content, and it was this failure to make his intentions clear that induced him to write his lengthy essay on the way it should be played. He wrote a similar, though much shorter essay on *Der Fliegende Holländer* at about the same time, and the passage on the delivery of the Dutchman's aria in the first act ('*Die Frist ist um*') gives a vivid picture of the scene as he saw it in his mind and wished it to be done on stage. The actor must succeed in arousing and maintaining a profound sympathy for the Dutchman, he declared, 'and this he will do if he follows precisely the following main outlines of the characterisation:

'His first entry is uncommonly grave and solemn: his hesitant slowness as he steps ashore should be in striking contrast to the mysteriously swift approach of his ship across the sea. During the low trumpet notes (B minor) at the very end of the introduction he has crossed a gangway, placed there by the crew, from the ship's deck to a flat rock on the shore: the first note of the aria's ritornello (the low E sharp of the double basses) accompanies his first step on to dry land. The wave-like phrase of the cellos and violas indicates musically the lurching gait customary to sailors coming ashore after a long sea voyage. With the first crotchets of the third bar he takes his second step, still with folded arms and lowered head; the third and fourth steps coincide with the notes of the eighth and tenth bars. From this point on his movements follow the dictates of the ensuing words, but the actor must never allow himself to be tempted into a lively pacing to and fro: a certain uncanny stillness in his outward bearing, even when giving the most intense emotional expression to his inner pain and despair, will most effectively convey the nature of his appearance. The first phrases are to be sung without any trace of emotion, as if in a state of utter exhaustion – and almost strictly in time, as indeed the whole recitative should be. The words "*Ha, stolzer Ozean!*, etc.", though sung with a grim bitterness, are still no truly passionate outburst: with a kind of hideous scorn he casts a glance back over the sea, only slightly turning his head. During the ritornello after "*doch ewig meine Qual*, etc." he lets his head sink down again, as if weary and sad, and he sings the words "*euch, des Weltmeers Fluten*, etc." staring straight ahead. I do not wish to restrict the singer's gestures in the allegro passage "*Wie oft in Meeres tiefsten Grund*, etc." too severely, but he should still keep within the bounds of my main instruction to preserve as much stillness as possible in his outward movements, however intense the passion and pain conveyed in his singing: a movement (not too sweeping) of the arm or hand should suffice for each sharp accent in the delivery. Even the words "*Niemals der Tod, nirgends ein Grab!*", which must of course be sung with the utmost emphasis, are still part of his *description* of his sufferings rather than a full and direct outburst of despair: that comes in the following passage, for which the greatest energy of expression must be reserved. With his repetition of the words "*dies der Verdammnis Schreckgebot!*" his head and his whole body have slumped, and he remains fixed in this position during the first four bars of the postlude. At the fifth bar of the violin tremolo (E flat) he raises his head towards the heavens, while the rest of his body remains slumped. With the entry of the soft drum-roll in the ninth bar of the postlude he is overcome by an awful shivering, his drooping hands clench convulsively and his lips tremble as finally, his staring eyes fixed throughout on the heavens, he begins the phrase "*Dich frage ich*, etc." This entire, almost direct address to "God's angel" must, though being sung with all possible intensity of expression, be delivered in the bodily position as previously described (with no change except at those points where the singing requires it): as, under frightful torment, he vents his rage against eternal justice, we must literally see before us a "fallen angel". With the words "*Vergeb'ne Hoffnung,* etc." the whole force of his despair finally bursts through: in fury he draws himself up and, impelled by the violence of his pain, his eyes still fixed on heaven, he thrusts all "fruitless hope" from him: he can no longer believe in his promised redemption, and (with the entry of the drum-roll and the double basses) he sinks down as if totally annihilated. With the entry of the allegro ritornello his features regain animation, as if he has found a new and terrible final hope – the hope that the world will end and he too necessarily perish. This final allegro demands the utmost energy in both vocal expression and gesture, for here his passion is unbridled. However, the singer should take care, despite the force of his delivery, to make this whole passage appear as a summoning of all his strength, which culminates, with the words "*Ihr Welten! endet euren Lauf!* etc.", in its strongest and most shattering outburst. Here the nobility of expression must reach its highest point. After the last words, "*ewige Vernichtung, nimm mich auf!*", he stands unmoving, almost like a statue, through the entire fortissimo of the postlude. Only with the entry of the pianissimo and the muffled singing from the ship's hold does his powerful bearing gradually relax. His arms sink to his sides, and during the four "espressivo" bars of the first violins he wearily lowers his head, then, during the last eight bars of the postlude, staggers towards the cliff face at his side: he leans his back against it and remains for a long time in this position, his arms folded across his chest.'

His reason for describing this scene in such detail, Wagner went on to say, was to show in what way he required his Dutchman to be presented and what weight should be attached to a very careful matching of the action to the music.

It was this kind of instruction that critics not unnaturally seized on to accuse Wagner of limiting his singers' proper freedom of expression, but he stuck stoutly to his assertion that he was simply holding up to them a picture to reproduce in their own way according to their natural instincts. There was a difference, he claimed, between imitation and reproduction, the first being just an inborn natural talent, and the second a conscious artistic use of that talent, which permitted actors to express something never before seen or experienced in their own lives, provided it was made sufficiently clear to them. He called this process 'setting the example'.

It was best done, of course, in person by the producer

rather than through written instructions to the actor–singers, and in his essay 'On Actors and Singers' Wagner cited the first production of *Die Meistersinger von Nürnberg* in 1868 as that which had given him his greatest inner satisfaction. 'I believe that with this work I demonstrated most clearly what I described earlier as "setting the example" to our actors, and, though a witty friend expressed the opinion that my orchestral score sounded to him like an unending fugue transformed into an opera, my solo and chorus singers on the other hand knew that in the course of solving their difficult musical tasks they had found their way through to a form of continuous dialogue which, once mastered, came to them as easily and naturally as the commonest of everyday speech.'

It can be argued that *Die Meistersinger* is, of all Wagner's works, the one closest in form and content to the *Singspiel* that was his avowed starting point, and that the style of singing and acting it demands differs greatly from that required in *Tristan und Isolde*, for example. Wagner's reply to this reservation would be that the differences are clearly indicated in both the words and the music, and the actor, having absorbed these, should have no difficulty in finding a way of presenting them in natural and credible human terms. This was the reason for his insistence that every participant in a stage production, from the musical director and stage designer down to chorus members and stage hands, should be involved in rehearsals from the very beginning, so that each of them would have a clear picture in his mind of the relevant significance of his own contribution to the final effect of the whole.

The shape rehearsals should take is described in meticulous detail in the essay on the production of *Tannhäuser*. They should begin with a reading of their parts by all the actors under the producer's direction and in the presence of the conductor and the members of the chorus, whose parts should be read by the chorus master or the chorus leader. The parts should be read aloud with their full dramatic emphasis, 'and if, either through lack of understanding or practice, an expressive effect, based on the text alone, is not immediately forthcoming, the rehearsal should be repeated until, through an understanding of the various situations and their place in the construction as a whole, the necessary expression is achieved.'

Only after completion of this stage should the singers turn their attention to the music: 'In the present state of opera they can scarcely be expected to remember that their prime responsibility is to be actors, and, in order not to confuse the means with the ends at the very start, they should not be allowed to concern themselves with the enhanced musical expression of their speech until their effectiveness as actors has been sufficiently prepared. Their normal habits might seem adequate for the products of most opera composers, but I must firmly declare that my works demand for their presentation a mode of practice in direct contrast to these. The singer who is incapable of reciting his "role" according to the demands of the *poet*, and with all the required expression, will certainly not be able to do justice to the demands of the *composer*, let alone portray the character he is playing. I believe so strongly in this assertion and insist so firmly on adherence to the conditions I have laid down regarding reading rehearsals that I am prepared to request, indeed to demand that, should these reading rehearsals fail to arouse in all participants a comprehensive interest in the subject and in the ways of presenting it on stage, my work should be put aside and the idea of producing it abandoned completely.'

This peremptory declaration, which might have frightened off many opera managers, did not in fact do so, for the simple reason that most of them did not bother to read the essay in which it was contained. *Tannhäuser* and *Lohengrin* continued to be played during Wagner's lifetime in productions which, on the few occasions he could be induced to see them, filled him with dismay. In his own productions – of *Tannhäuser* and *Lohengrin* as well as the later works – he faithfully followed the rehearsal methods he laid down in that early essay. The emphasis, as one sees, is primarily on acting ability, and it brought him face to face with a practical dilemma that he never managed fully to overcome: a good actor was not always a good singer, and a good singer was not always a good actor. Which, when choice was limited, should he choose?

The singer against whom he measured all others was Wilhelmine Schröder-Devrient, who for him was the 'example' behind his whole artistic development. Having impressed Weber in her performance as Agathe in *Der Freischütz* and Beethoven as Leonore in *Fidelio* before she was twenty years of age, she was a celebrated soprano when as a very young man Wagner saw her for the first time in Leipzig, and she became a friend and wise counsellor during his years as conductor in Dresden, playing under his direction Adriano in *Rienzi*, Senta in *Der Fliegende Holländer* and Venus in *Tannhäuser*, though now nearing the end of her career. She died in 1860, and Wagner dedicated his essay 'On Actors and Singers' to her memory. Her image figures as 'Ancient Tragedy' in the sgraffito he put on the wall of his house Wahnfried in Bayreuth. He wrote of her in his essay: 'The question has repeatedly been put to me whether, since she was celebrated as a singer, her *voice* was really so remarkable – as if this were in such a case all that mattered. I have always found it thoroughly vexing to have to answer this question, because I was annoyed at seeing this great tragedienne being put up for comparison with the effeminate castrati of our opera houses. Were anyone now to put the same question to me, I should reply more or less as follows: No, she had no "voice" at all, but she had such superb breath control and was able through this to give such wonderful expression to a truly feminine soul that one had no thoughts to spare for either singing or voice . . .

'I owe all my knowledge of the nature of the actor's essential being to this great woman, and from what she taught me I have also been enabled to identify the basic element of this essential being: it is *truthfulness*. The art of noble deception practised by the born actor is not to be won through mendacity, and this is the dividing line between the genuine mimic artist and the bad play-actor, whom modern taste has made a habit of showering with gold and with laurels . . . Schröder-Devrient would have sunk down in shame at the thought of earning a round of applause by the use of a false effect.'

The only other singer to arouse in Wagner such undiluted veneration was the tenor, Ludwig Schnorr von Carolsfeld, who was also honoured with a place (representing 'Germanic Myth') on the Wahnfried sgraffito. Wagner was at first prejudiced against him on account of his corpulence, but his first sight of him on stage (in Karlsruhe in 1862 as Lohengrin) converted him at once. He described his feelings in his essay 'My Memories of Ludwig Schnorr von Carolsfeld' ('*Meine Erinnerungen an Ludwig Schnorr von Carolsfeld*'), written in 1868, three years after Schnorr's death at the early age of twenty-nine: 'If the sight of the Swan Knight stepping ashore from his little boat conveyed at first sight a somewhat alienating impression of how a young Heracles should look, nevertheless I was at once conscious of that sense of magic inherent in that heaven-sent legendary hero that leads one not to ask, "How does he look?", but to tell oneself, "This is he." This instantaneous effect, striking to the very soul, can only be compared with magic: I remember having received it from the great Schröder-Devrient in my earliest youth, and it influenced the course of my whole life. Never since then, till Ludwig Schnorr's appearance as Lohengrin, did it affect me so strangely and so powerfully. In the course of his performance I soon recognised certain immaturities in his interpretation and presentation of his role, but even these conveyed to me the charm of an unspoilt youthful purity, a chaste promise of a splendid artistic blossoming.'

A few months later, at home in Biebrich, Wagner went through the role of Tristan with Schnorr, and the singer voiced his doubts regarding the stageability of the third act: 'He admitted to me that these doubts were based less on fears of a possible strain on his voice and his physical powers than on his failure to grasp the significance of a single phrase, which he realised to be of the greatest importance: the curse on love, and especially the musical expression of the words from "*aus Lachen und Weinen, Wonnen und Wunden*" onwards. I showed him how I intended it to be, and what tremendous emphasis I wished to be put on this phrase. He swiftly understood and saw that he had gone wrong in judging the musical tempo, which he had taken too fast; his consequent hurrying of this passage was, he now realised, to blame for his failure to find the right expression for it and thus also for his misunderstanding. I asked him to bear in mind that, in demanding a slower tempo, I was putting an unwonted, indeed a tremendous strain on his voice, but he dismissed this as of little concern and at once proved to me how, as a direct consequence of drawing the phrase out, he was able to sing it to our complete satisfaction. This one feature is for me as unforgettable as it has been instructive. Great physical exertion ceased to be felt as onerous with the singer's awareness of the correct expression of the passage: intellectual understanding immediately provided the strength to overcome the material difficulty.'

When *Tristan* came to be produced on stage in Munich in 1865 Wagner found Schnorr already so versed in his role that there was little he needed to do: 'Not a single thread of this soul's fabric, not the very smallest hint of a hidden relationship which had escaped him and to which he did not respond with the utmost delicacy. Thus it was only a matter of paying the closest attention to the technical means of expression of the singer, musician and actor in order to achieve a complete blend of personal talents and their inherent qualities with the ideal representation of the subject.'

There were other singers for whom he found words of praise. Schnorr's wife Malvina, who sang Isolde in that first production, he even compared, in a letter written during rehearsals to King Ludwig (28 April 1865), with Wilhelmine Schröder-Devrient: 'From her one will be able to learn what a tragedienne is!' Anton Mitterwurzer, who had been the first singer to appreciate and respond to his ideals as Wolfram in the first production of *Tannhäuser* twenty years earlier, was rewarded in *Tristan* with the part of Kurwenal. And for Joseph Tichatschek, his first Tannhäuser, he retained a warm regard – not for his acting talent, but for the expressive qualities of his voice: where, he once asked, was there another singer who could deliver Lohengrin's farewell to the swan (*'Nun sei bedankt, mein lieber Schwan'*) with 'the graceful hint of a trembling smile in his voice' – a detail 'that costs so little effort and touches and bewitches the heart'?

However, none of these singers was available to him when, his ideal theatre now built in Bayreuth, he set about the task of staging *Der Ring des Nibelungen*, and his search for suitable singers involved him in months of travel, auditions and correspondence. It would take too long to chronicle all the hopes and disappointments culminating in the assembly of a cast that in several instances proved far from ideal. My intention here is rather to identify the qualities that Wagner demanded (and still demands) from his actor-singers than to catalogue his own personal successes or failures. But there is something to be learnt about the extent of his demands from an account of his efforts with Georg Unger, his first Siegfried.

Unger, chosen after several other candidates for the role had been tried and rejected, was not widely known, though he had been singing for some years and was already in his mid-thirties (quite an advanced age for singers in those days). Wagner chose him, firstly, because of his youthful and virile appearance, and secondly, because he detected in the voice, heard only in vocal exercises, a potential beauty of expression like that he had so much prized in Tichatschek. He had, however, acquired certain bad habits in his voice production, and Wagner, at his own expense, put him in the hands of a music teacher in Munich, Julius Hey.

The story of their struggle with their willing, though not outstandingly gifted pupil is entertainingly and instructively told by Hey in his book *Richard Wagner als Vortragsmeister*, (Leipzig, 1911). Before starting on Unger's grooming Wagner explained the nature of his ideal young Siegfried. He must be sturdy and well-built, thus revealing his godly ancestry; he must have a naturally strong and resilient voice with a free delivery, but capable of great modulation; he must pronounce his words with the utmost clarity; he should have the fresh and at the same time level-headed outlook of the budding man of action. The singer's own native temperament should be similar, but in addition he should have sufficient insight to appreciate the deeper implications of his role. He should have a natural acting ability and a very expressive face.

Wagner chose Siegfried's '*Hei-a-ho! Ha-ha!*' as he forges the sword Nothung in the first act as the subject of his first practical lesson. This, he said, was more in the nature of a merry shout, such as might be heard daily in the Bavarian mountains from an exuberant young timber-feller: there should be nothing at all artistic about it. But in Act Two, where young Siegfried's character undergoes its greatest development, the lessons became more complicated. A short passage of less than two bars yielded, on Unger's first attempt, three mistakes. '*Hier soll ich das Fürchten lernen?*' ('Here, then, shall this fear be taught me?'*): Unger, Hey tells us, began softly on '*Hier*', increased his volume for the D flat of '*Fürchten*' and emphasised the last syllable of '*lernen*' on the rising sixth. Wagner explained to him how it should be done: 'The "*Hier*" should be mezzoforte, an expression of surprise and curiosity; the "*Fürchten*" must not be given any particular significance, since at this point Siegfried does not know what the word "fear" means; and the last syllable of "*lernen*" should not be stressed.'

In the first meeting with the Woodbird, when Siegfried cannot yet understand its language, he is still a curious child, and his voice must sound as if it were in a higher register: bright and friendly – it is just a pleasant chat. But with Fafner's entry Siegfried's tone becomes bold and cheeky, and it should imply a confident awareness of his superiority over the fearsome dragon. 'It should sound,' Wagner said, 'like the sword Nothung flashing in the bright sunshine.'

After the killing of Fafner and the Woodbird's warning,

---

* This and the following quotations from the *Ring* translated by Andrew Porter.

Siegfried becomes aware of a new feeling in his relationship with Mime. It is no longer just a subconscious repugnance, but a definite suspicion. This is the point, Wagner explained, at which the border is crossed between carefree childhood and consciously directed will. In his dialogue with the dissembling dwarf Siegfried must at the outset be cautious and contained, his words sharply articulated. When Mime offers him a drink, the simple question, *'Wie hast du diesen gebraut?'* ('But say how this one was brewed'), should express the suspicion more openly, but it is only with the last question, *'Im Schlafe willst du mich morden?'* ('While I'm sleeping you plan to kill me?'), that the full repugnance breaks through. The question should start in a veiled tone and open out increasingly until the last word *'morden'*, which should be full of horror.

The weariness after the battle with Fafner and the altercation with Mime, Wagner said, should be reflected in the voice, which can legitimately sound weary. It begins to take on colour again only when the Woodbird tells Siegfried of the sleeping Brünnhilde, and the youth feels the first stirrings of love in his heart. He questions the bird with increasing urgency, though his final vital question – will he be able to penetrate the fire that surrounds Brünnhilde? – is broader, betraying his apprehension. After the Woodbird's reply he echoes its notes in a bright, exultant voice: *'Der dumme Knab', der das Fürchten nicht kennt, mein Vöglein, der bin ja ich!'* ('A foolish boy, unacquainted with fear, dear Woodbird, why, that's me!')

This is a graphic illustration, not only of what Wagner demanded of his singers, but of the way in which in practice he set about making clear to them just *why* he demanded it. Another book written by an eyewitness, Heinrich Porges's *Die Bühnenproben zu den Bayreuther Festspielen des Jahres 1876*, confirms that this was his normal habit, not only with beginners such as Unger, but with seasoned singers such as Albert Niemann (Siegmund) and Franz Betz (Wotan) as well. Behind his exertions there was always the one single thought: the drama was paramount, and everyone concerned in it had the duty of understanding it and remaining true to it, even at the cost to the singer of sacrificing what he most prized in himself: beauty of tone. His advice to his Siegfried to shout his '*Hei-a-ho! Ha-ha!*' and to sound weary after his encounters with Fafner and Mime is in line with his declaration to Niemann at the time of the production of *Tannhäuser* in Paris that it would be 'no great misfortune' for the singer to sound hoarse in the 'Rome Narration' in the third act, since at the time the hero is exhausted, starved and at the end of his wits. On the other hand, he welcomed sheer beauty of tone when it was making a dramatic point, as in Tichatschek's farewell to the swan in *Lohengrin*.

In spite of his emphasis on dramatic truthfulness, Wagner was nevertheless not blind to the technical difficulties under which singers worked, and he paid particular attention to the matter of breath control, the quality that he singled out for special praise in his assessment of Wilhelmine Schröder-Devrient. He wrote in his essay 'On Actors and Singers' of the inability of most German singers to pronounce words as they are normally spoken, with the result that neither they nor the audience understand what they are saying, let alone why they are saying it. Convinced as he was that the effect of his dramas depended as much on the words as on the music, he laid particular stress in rehearsals on enunciation. In his account of the production of *Parsifal* in Bayreuth in 1882 he wrote of the contrasts of style the work demands, ranging from the ceremonial and the devout to 'the strongly passionate, rough, indeed wild' passages, and he described the attempts he and his singers made to deal with them: 'Above all, attention had to be paid to the greatest clarity, starting with the words. A passionate phrase is bound to make a confusing, even an alienating effect when its logical content remains incomprehensible. To enable us to take this in without effort, it is imperative that we should at once understand the tiniest part of every sentence: an omitted prefix, a swallowed suffix, a neglected connecting syllable – these immediately destroy the necessary comprehensibility. And this same neglect also has a direct effect on the melody itself, of which, because of the disappearance of the musical particles, only isolated accents remain. The more passionate the phrase, the more it tends to sound like a mere vocal ejaculation, and the effect of this, when heard at a distance from which none of the connecting syllables reaches our ears at all, is curious, not to say ridiculous . . . When, at rehearsals of the *Ring* dramas six years ago, an emphatic recommendation was made to give the "small" notes preference over the "large", this was in the interests of clarity, without which both drama and music, both speech and melody remain incomprehensible . . .

'Outbursts of passionate suffering demand the use of an extreme degree of violence. That is of course an essential part of any profoundly tragic subject, as is the necessity of giving vent to it, but it can produce its shattering effect only when this extreme degree is kept throughout within the bounds of emotional expression. The surest way of achieving this we found to be through a prudent economy of breathing as well as of pliant movement. We came to realise during our rehearsal exercises to what extent we were guilty in opera singing of wastefulness, above all of our breath, and soon saw what a single, well-controlled breath could do to invest a row of notes with their proper melodic and logical sense by preserving their relationship to one another. Merely by prudent preservation and distribution of a breath's power we discovered how easy and natural it was to do justice to what I have called the "small" notes (usually in a lower register) in their important function as links within both speech and melody. This was because we were obliged to guard against a wasteful expenditure of breath on the higher notes (which anyway stand out by themselves), knowing to what extent the complete phrase would gain by being sung within the same single breath. Thus we were able to sustain long melodic lines unbroken, even when they contained a large variety of emotional accents and vocal colourings. As eloquent examples I might remind our audiences of Kundry's fairly lengthy account of Herzeleide's fate in the second act and Gurnemanz's description of Good Friday magic in the third.'

The two examples Wagner chose to illustrate his point are not in fact those that cause most concern to the audience if the words are indistinguishable, since the sheer beauty of the music is enough to carry them through. There are other passages in all the works where the singer's inability to project his words can prove a greater trial: Gurnemanz's expositions in the first act of *Parsifal*, Wotan's narration in the second act of *Die Walküre* and David's music lesson to Walther in the first act of *Die Meistersinger*, to give just three instances. But, even when the music is at its most beautiful, one knows by experience how much its effect is enriched by a clear understanding of the words. Each of us has probably had the good fortune in years of opera-going to encounter a few singers who enunciate their words clearly with no loss of singing tone, which suggests that those who do not are impelled by wilful negligence rather than genuine disability. Perhaps, however – to be more charitable – they do not know how to achieve the necessary clarity of diction, and in that case the technical solution offered by Wagner himself in the above quotation may prove of help. Now that he is no longer with us to bully and cajole, we are dependent for enlightenment on the written instructions he left behind, in numerous essays as in the scores of his works themselves. In their mixture of valid reasoning, interpretative hints and practical advice they provide a valuable substitute, and certainly, as far as actor-singers are concerned, a model well worth studying.

I Still Owe the World *Tannhäuser*:
The Dresden and Paris Versions

My aim in this book has been not just to identify Wagner's ideas on drama at all levels from spiritual and moral aspects down to techniques of acting and breath control, but also to show how vital and essential a part these ideas played in the actual creation of his dramatic works. The final two chapters, in which I follow the composer through the development of two of these works from the moment of their conception to their final realisation on stage, should serve to emphasise the point, if in completely different ways. *Tannhäuser*, written before his theoretical ideas were fully formulated, caused Wagner much concern throughout his life as he strove to find a form worthy of it. *Parsifal*, written after his ideas had been put to the test with his production of the *Ring* at Bayreuth, is both a final statement and a new beginning.

'I still owe the world *Tannhäuser*': Wagner's remark to his wife Cosima, recorded in her diary on 23 January 1883, less than a month before his death, leaves open the question whether he was thinking only of a model production of the work or of a further rewriting of it. Certainly he intended a new production at Bayreuth: it was to be the first of his older works to be presented in his theatre there, and Cosima wrote in her diary on 5 February 1883, 'He says that if he can get this settled, he will have achieved more than by staging *Tristan*.'

Wagner took an active part in several productions of *Tannhäuser*, beginning with the very first in Dresden in 1845, then in Zurich (1855), in Paris (1861) and finally in Vienna (1875), this last including the new music he had composed for the Paris production. Add to these a single performance of the earlier Dresden version in Munich, for which he personally rehearsed Ludwig Schnorr von Carolsfeld – achieving what he described in his reminiscence of that singer as a complete realisation of his innermost artistic purpose – and one might conclude that Wagner had already had ample opportunity to demonstrate to the world how he wished to see it staged.

His continued dissatisfaction with the work suggests therefore that he had still further improvements in view, and that these would have been of a much more radical nature than his previous changes is indicated in an earlier reference in Cosima's diaries. It is dated 6 November 1877, when she wrote: 'In the evening went through the first act of *Tannhäuser* with Herr [Anton] Seidl; R. says he has in mind shortening the new first scene [the Paris version of the Venusberg] considerably, it weighs the rest down too much, there is a lack of balance, this scene goes beyond the style of *Tannhäuser* as a whole. – I argue in its defence, saying that it casts over the audience the magic spell which causes Tannhäuser's downfall, and thus it makes the 2nd act more understandable; it is also fitting that the magic underworld is different from the simple world above. "That is what I told myself," R. observes, "but it is not right." – The problem occupies him greatly.'

The theme, as in all Wagner's works, is the longing for perfect love. In *Der Fliegende Holländer* the accent lies entirely on the spiritual side of love, the power of a woman 'faithful unto death' to redeem a man afflicted by a curse; there is no sign of any sensual feeling between Senta and the Dutchman. In *Tannhäuser* sensuality is very much to the fore as an inescapable part of mortal existence, but the gist of the argument is that the physical side of love is not enough in itself: the spiritual also demands its due. In his 'Communication' Wagner expressed his disgust with the lust for frivolous enjoyment in both art and love that characterised the world in which he lived. *Tannhäuser* had been an attempt to define his yearning for 'a rarer, nobler element . . . an unending, unearthly love that appeared attainable only in death . . . a true love that, though indeed springing from the soil of absolute sensuality . . . can never be satisfied on the repellent plane of modern sensuality.'

Tannhäuser's search for a perfect love of this kind, not in death, but in life, leads him into disaster through his egocentric approach: his failure to recognise before it is too late that love involves more than one person. It is in his relationship with Elisabeth that the drama lies.

A clearer picture of this relationship emerges in the lengthy guide to future presenters of his work which Wagner wrote in 1852 in Switzerland, after his banishment from Saxony had effectively cut off any opportunity of supervising personally new productions of *Tannhäuser* in German theatres. In his essay, entitled 'On the Performing of *Tannhäuser*', Wagner wrote a penetrating character study of his hero: 'As the most essential feature of this character I point to the always directly active, almost excessive way in which he is gripped by the emotions of each particular situation in which he finds himself at any one time, and the lively contrast in the expression of the emotions to which the violent changes in the situation give rise. Tannhäuser is never in any circumstances "slightly" anything, but always fully and to the utmost. He has lain in Venus's arms with the greatest delight; in the clearest recognition of the necessity of tearing himself free from her he breaks the bonds that bind him to the goddess of love, without in any way despising her. With complete abandon he savours the overwhelming impression of the world of Nature to which he has returned, the familiar confines of long-accustomed emotions, the tearful outburst of a childlike feeling of religious remorse. His cry, "Almighty, praise to thee! Great are the marvels of thy mercy!", is the involuntary expression of a feeling that takes irresistible possession of his innermost heart. So strong and so genuine is this emotion and his awareness of the need for reconciliation with the world – a world perceived in its largest and broadest sense – that he timidly and evasively recoils from the meeting with his former companions and their offers of forgiveness: his desire is not simply for a return to his former habits, but for progress towards something as great and as noble as his newly-gained perception of the world has revealed to him. This nameless something that alone matches his present emotion suddenly takes form when he hears the name "Elisabeth". With lightning speed, past and future flow together within him like a stream of fire that, as he learns of Elisabeth's love for him, transforms itself into a shining star, leading him towards a new life. Wholly in the grip of this newest emotion, which he has never before experienced, he rises up in blissful joy and storms off in search of his beloved. All that has happened in the past seems to him like a dull and distant dream that he can scarcely even recall: he is aware of one thing only, of a fair maiden, a sweet virgin who loves him; and in this love, in his response to it, he recognises only one thing: the raging, all-consuming fire of life. With this same fire, this same fervour he had once enjoyed Venus's love, and instinctively he must fulfil the oath he freely made to her on parting – to be henceforth her bold champion against all the world.

'This world loses no time in throwing down its challenge.

Here, where pride makes the sacrifice weakness demands of it, the individual finds justification for his existence only through recognition of the unending need to adjust the communication of his instinctive feelings to the overruling demands of custom. Tannhäuser, who is capable of expressing his most deeply held instinctive emotions only in a thoroughly uncompromising way, must inevitably find himself completely at odds with this world, and he is emotionally so aware of this that, in the interests of his own existence, it becomes a matter of life and death to him to join battle with his adversary. This single necessity takes complete possession of him when the singers' contest brings the matter into open conflict. Rising to it, he forgets all around him, throws all consideration to the winds. Yet when at last he loudly and clearly proclaims himself Venus's champion, in his feelings he is solely defending his love for Elisabeth. At this point he is standing on the utmost heights of his life-loving instincts, and nothing can shatter the sublime rapture with which, single-handed, he defies an entire world except for one thing, utterly new to him and hitherto unsuspected, of which he now suddenly becomes fully aware: the emergence of a woman who for love of him sacrifices herself. Surfeited with bliss in Venus's arms, he had longed for – pain. This profoundly human yearning has led him to the woman who now *suffers* with him, whereas Venus had only shared delight with him. His wish has been granted, and from now on he cannot live without sufferings just as intense as his former delights had been. Yet these sufferings are neither sought nor voluntarily assumed: the irresistible force with which they have invaded his heart are the result of fellow-feeling, which now, through the energy of his character, nourishes his suffering to the point of self-destruction. And it is here that the tremendous difference between his love for Elisabeth and his love for Venus finds expression. He cannot bear to meet Elisabeth's gaze, each word she utters cuts his heart like a sword: all he can do is to seek through his own torments to atone to her for the torments she is enduring out of love for him, even if it will be granted to him alone, in the final moments of a painful death in distant lands, to know that atonement has been made.

'What suffering would he not now embrace with joy? Before the eyes of a world that a moment before, in jubilant victory, he had confronted as a mortal enemy, he now throws himself with willing fervour in the dust, for the world to trample beneath its feet. Thus he is in no way akin to the pilgrims who undertake easy penances for the sake of their own salvation: it is "to sweeten the tears of the angel who wept for the sinner" that amid frightful torments he seeks the path to his salvation, since this salvation can lie only in the knowledge that the tears that were shed for him have been sweetened. We must accept his claim that no other pilgrim has ever sought salvation with such fervour; but the more genuine and wholehearted his remorse, his feelings of penance and desire for absolution, the more overwhelming must his loathing be for the mendacity and heartlessness that stand revealed at the end of his pilgrimage! In view of the sublime truthfulness of his emotions, which were centred, not on himself and his own salvation, but on his love for another being and thus on this beloved being herself, it is inevitable that his hatred of a world that would have to change its course before it could exonerate both him and love itself bursts into roaring flames, and it is these flames that sear his despairing heart. When he returns from Rome, his emotion is one of fury against a world that, on account of the sublime integrity of his feelings, denies him the right to live. It is not a yearning for lustful enjoyment that causes him to seek the Venusberg again, but his hatred of a world for which he can feel nothing but contempt. Despair is driving him to the place where he can hide himself away from the gaze of the "angel", to sweeten whose tears the whole world can offer no balm.

'Such is the nature of his love for Elisabeth, and it is this love that she returns. What the whole world of custom was unable to offer she gave by including her lover, despite the world's disapproval, in her prayers and, in the divine awareness of the force of her death, by pardoning the sinner as she died. As he too dies, Tannhäuser thanks her for the sublime favour of love she has thus bestowed on him. None of those standing beside his corpse could fail to envy him, and each of them, the whole world, even God himself, must needs call him blessed.'

Within this character study of his hero Wagner effectively revealed the whole theme and substance of his drama, and in his guide he dealt only briefly and in hardly more than practical terms with its other leading protagonists: Venus, Elisabeth and Wolfram: 'Venus in particular,' he wrote, 'can succeed only if, beside a favourable outward disposition, she is able to believe completely in her role, and this she will achieve if she manages to consider Venus as wholly justified in all she proclaims, and justified to the extent that she yields only to the woman who sacrifices herself for the sake of love. For Elisabeth, on the other hand, the difficulty is that the actress must convey the impression of a very youthful and virginal ingenuousness, without revealing too soon the very experienced, delicate feminine feeling that in the end makes her capable of fulfilling her task.' As for Tannhäuser's friend Wolfram, who is also in love with Elisabeth, 'the less violent demands of his sensual urges enable him to turn living impressions into subjects for the reflections of a thinking mind. He is thus predominantly a poet and an artist, whereas Tannhäuser is first and foremost a human being.'

After reading all this one can hardly be in any doubt that the main theme of *Tannhäuser*, expressed in bald terms, is the necessity and difficulty of achieving a balance between the demands of physical love and spiritual love, demonstrated in the story of a full-blooded male and a timid virgin who, brought up in a world of conventional prudery, is ashamed of her sexual feelings. Elisabeth's courageous act in placing herself between Tannhäuser and the swords of the outraged knights is the moment of full recognition between them, and the moment when their own feelings about their love for each other undergo a radical change: it forces her to acknowledge without fear the implications of physical love, and it forces him to become aware for the first time of the validity of a spiritual love that goes beyond a mere gratification of the senses. From this point on their concern is for each other, no longer just for their separate selves.

Tannhäuser, as Wagner constantly emphasised in his guide, does not see himself as a sinner. His remorse is not for having succumbed to his natural urges, but for having caused his beloved to suffer by his insensitive mauling of her still undeveloped sexual instincts. Thus it must have jarred on Wagner to hear his own wife Cosima speak of 'the magic spell which causes Tannhäuser's downfall'. There was no magic spell involved: the physical urges presided over by Venus are a natural and essential part of human existence. And there was no downfall, except in the sense that Tannhäuser was banished from courtly society and refused absolution by the Pope with the harsh words that he had as much chance of redemption as his staff had of sprouting leaves. If *Tannhäuser* is to be regarded as a tragedy at all, it is in the sense that *Romeo and Juliet* is a tragedy: the story of a pair of lovers who are separated from each other and hounded to their deaths by rigid social conventions. 'See what a scourge is laid upon your hate,' says Prince Escalus, 'that heaven finds means to kill your joys with love!' Shakespeare's final summing-up is matched by Wagner with the return of the young pilgrims from Rome, after both Elisabeth and Tannhäuser are dead, with the news that the Pope's staff had broken into leaf.

What might be called the Roman Catholic view of *Tann-häuser* as the story of a redeemed sinner dogged it from the very start. It has proved remarkably persistent, even in devoted Wagnerian circles, Catholic and non-Catholic, as Cosima's remarks show. She must have forgotten at the time she made them Wagner's castigation in his 'Communication to my Friends' of critics 'grown bright in modern dissoluteness who read into my *Tannhäuser* a specifically Christian tendency, impotently raising its arms to heaven.' But, if they were wrong, it is surely fair to ask to what extent Wagner himself, in the way he shaped his work, was responsible for the misunderstanding.

A reading of the text provides no grounds for reproach. There we find all the characteristics of his hero as described in his guide fully and economically planted. Tannhäuser's first words, amid the sensual delights of the Venusberg, are, 'Too much! Too much! Oh, that I might now awake!', and his loyal attempt to pacify Venus with his song in praise of erotic love breaks down at once with a relapse into nostalgia for the world outside: 'Though gods may enjoy eternal bliss, I am in thrall to change. Pleasure is not my sole desire: in the midst of joy I long for pain. From this thy realm I must flee. Oh, queen of love, goddess, set me free!' Venus responds with alternate bouts of anger, cajolery, threats and forebodings, to which Tannhäuser momentarily succumbs, only to return to his resolve to leave her realm, though not to desert her cause.

Thus when, by uttering the name of the Virgin Mary, he finally banishes Venus and finds himself back in the world of Nature and of men (a contrast skilfully pinpointed by the innocent song of a shepherd boy and the pious strains of passing pilgrims), Tannhäuser has established himself as a hero well worthy of our interest, if not entirely of our sympathy. Sympathy begins to stir only when we witness his hesitation in accepting the overtures of friendship from the Landgrave and his minstrels, his former companions: 'Peace to you all, and let me go my way.' Tannhäuser is clearly a man of conscience, no mere Don Juan. But that he is also a man of strong impulses, as he has already shown in his rejection of Venus, is once more brought to our attention by the swiftness with which, on hearing of Elisabeth's love for him, he changes his mind and agrees to rejoin the Landgrave's court. We are left wondering, as the curtain falls on the first act, what will happen next. It is an exemplary exposition.

Wagner wastes no time in involving us in the central drama. Elisabeth's joy at the return of her favourite minstrel at the beginning of the second act, the artless manner with which she confesses her love for him, swiftly establish her in our consciousness, not as a saint, but as a person of flesh and blood, as yet untouched and unawakened. Her innocent question to Tannhäuser, 'Heinrich, what hast thou done to me?' provides him with grounds for believing that her conception of love, if not yet fully understood by herself, might be closer to his than to that of the seemingly bloodless beings among whom she has been brought up. And so in the ensuing singers' contest it appears to be: listening to Wolfram likening love to a pure spring that should not be stirred 'in wanton mood', she responds sympathetically to Tannhäuser's rejoinder that the spring is there to be drunk from. She does not express her agreement in words, but Wagner has put it in a stage direction: 'Elisabeth makes a movement indicating her approval, but, since all the other listeners remain earnestly silent, she shyly holds back.' Whether Tannhäuser notices this gesture we are not told. Almost certainly not, for in *My Life* Wagner tells of his horror when, at the first performance in Dresden, he saw his Tannhäuser go up to Elisabeth and direct his hymn of praise to Venus – in which in his 'mad ecstasy' he should be oblivious of his surroundings – 'with voluptuous tenderness' straight into her face. Tannhäuser's immediate reaction to the drawn swords of the outraged knights is, according to the stage direction, one of defiance, and it is only when Elisabeth, bravely placing herself between him and the knights, utters the words, 'Look on me, the maiden whose bloom he has shattered at a stroke,' that he becomes aware of the injury he has done her. The stage direction here is: 'Tannhäuser, emerging gradually from his exalted mood of excitement and defiance, is violently affected by Elisabeth's pleas for him, and he breaks down in remorseful sorrow.' His following words, according to Wagner's guide, 'contain the whole core of Tannhäuser's future existence': it is the moment in which he becomes conscious of the real dilemma of love, both physical and spiritual – the need to give as well as to receive:

'To lead the sinner to salvation
God's messenger came to me;
Yet, oh, in sacrilege to touch her,
I raised my wanton eyes to her!
Oh, thou, who high above this world of mortals
Sent me the angel of my grace,
Have mercy on me, who, deep in sinning,

So shamefully mistook heaven's mediator.'

As Elisabeth vows to devote her future life to praying for
him, Tannhäuser sets out for Rome in the hope of becoming
reconciled to the angel who, so rudely rebuffed, is still ready
to sacrifice herself for him.

That Tannhäuser is seeking absolution from the Pope for
Elisabeth's sake rather than for his own is established more
clearly in the third act, when he returns from Rome, his
hopes of sweetening the tears of his angel now destroyed by
the Pope's curse. Before his arrival we are given a moving
glimpse of Elisabeth, forlornly searching among the returning
pilgrims for the man she loves. The comprehensive nature of
her love is clearly expressed in the two last verses of her prayer
to the Virgin after her search has proved vain:

> 'Whenever, gripped in foolish madness,
> My heart has turned from thee –
> Whenever a sinful desire,
> A worldly yearning rose in me,
> I fought amid a host of suffering
> To kill it within my heart.
>
> Could I not atone for that remissness,
> Take me graciously in thy care,
> That, with humble greetings,
> I may approach you as a worthy maid,
> Only to beg the richest favour
> Of thy mercy towards *his* guilt.'

Again it is necessary to look to the stage direction for a clue
to Elisabeth's feelings towards the other man who loves
her. Wolfram, who has been watching unseen, now comes

forward, and she gestures to him not to speak. As he shyly asks whether he might accompany her back to the Wartburg, 'she expresses to him, again through gestures, that she thanks him with all her heart for his loyal love, but her path is leading her towards heaven, where she has an important task to perform; in consequence he should allow her to go unaccompanied, and not follow her.' Wolfram sadly watches her depart before taking up his harp and singing his lament to the evening star.

The dramatic contrast between this elegiac night scene and the arrival of Tannhäuser in his ragged pilgrim's cloak, his face pale and distorted, is as great as that of which it is a mirror image: his rapt emergence from the Venusberg into the springtime valley of the Wartburg in the first act. And his chilling account of the reception he received in Rome makes one wonder how Catholics could possibly regard this work as a glorification of their religion. The genuineness of Tannhäuser's remorse is so convincingly expressed that the Pope's rejection of his plea arouses the same sense of injustice in our emotions as it does in Tannhäuser's own, allowing us to look with sympathetic understanding on his urge to escape from the false promises of a hypocritical world to the sweet comforts of Venus's court.

The over-compressed succession of events leading to the conclusion of the work – Wolfram's struggle with Venus for Tannhäuser, Elisabeth's death and funeral, Tannhäuser's death and the return of the young pilgrims from Rome with news of the sprouting papal staff signifying his redemption – betrays the only signs of uncertainty (in execution rather than intention) in a text that is otherwise a shining example of compactness.

This was also Wagner's own opinion. He wrote from Paris to Mathilde Wesendonck in August 1860, while preparing for his production of *Tannhäuser* there: 'I had to acknowledge to myself that the text itself could not have been better done. It is rather in the music that I can improve things.'

Why did he feel the need to 'improve things' musically? *Tannhäuser*, after an admittedly shaky start in Dresden – due to inadequacies on the production side for which he was willing to accept at least a part of the blame – had gone on to achieve an ever-growing popularity, and by 1860 it was firmly established in the repertory of most German opera houses and not a few abroad. Most composers would have been content with such success, but Wagner was uneasy in the knowledge that his opera was being enjoyed, not for its psychological insights, but solely on account of its ravishing melodies, which at a superficial level more than made up for any supposed deficiencies in the story line. And, though it might once have been sweet to the ears of a budding young composer to hear his 'Pilgrims' Chorus' whistled by a swimmer in the river Elbe outside Dresden, this was not the kind of success at which, even at the time of writing *Tannhäuser*, he had been aiming.

At no time did Wagner despise melody or dispute its validity as a dramatic device. In his youth, he wrote in 'A Communication to my Friends', his ambition had been to invent 'truly original melodies that should bear a particular stamp peculiar to myself', and his preference lay always in the direction of 'broad, long sustained melodies'. His efforts to achieve a form of drama in which audiences would feel emotionally involved throughout led him, however, increasingly to abandon the idea of melody for its own sake. His task was now 'to present speech, according to its emotional content, in such a way that not the melodic expression itself, but the emotion expressed in it should arouse the listener's sympathy. The melody, therefore, must arise entirely of its own accord out of the speech; as pure melody it should attract no attention at all, or at best only to the extent that it is the most sensuous expression of the feeling revealed in the speech.'

His appreciation of the function of melody in relation to the words, he went on, had been more the result of instinct than of conscious reflection, and he admitted to having allowed his former preference for broad melody for its own sake to gain the upper hand at times in both *Der Fliegende Holländer* and *Tannhäuser*. This he attributed in part to the fact that he had not yet found a way to achieve a balance between words and music that would enable each to sustain the other without artificiality on either side.

Beside the 'Pilgrims' Chorus' there are doubtless passages in *Tannhäuser* in which the music engages the attention more than the words underlying them: for example, Tannhäuser's hymn of praise to Venus, the minstrels' '*O kehr' zurück, du kühner Sänger*', Elisabeth's '*Dich, teure Halle*' and Wolfram's '*O du, mein holder Abendstern*'. If in these Wagner was rash in allowing melody to run away with him and upset the balance, he was equally rash in the other direction in two passages in which he allowed the words to take precedence over the music. These are the singers' contest in the second act and Elisabeth's prayer in the third. Of the first Wagner wrote in *My Life*: 'In the conception of this scene I found myself unconsciously facing the dilemma in which I was obliged to make a decision for all time. Should this singers' contest be a concert of arias or a poetically dramatic competition? The nature of operatic tradition demanded . . . that here there should be a comparison and confrontation of evolutions in the art of singing, and that, in purely musical terms, the various vocal pieces should set each other off entertainingly by the use of markedly variegated rhythms and measures, in the same way that, for example, in a concert programme care must be taken to ensure that interest is kept alive by continual surprise, invoked by the utmost variety. This was not at all my intention. What I was really striving for, and doing my best to achieve, was to force the audience – for the very first time in opera – to participate in a poetic thought by following it through all phases of its development. Only in this way can the ensuing catastrophe be properly understood. It arises from no outward cause, but has to be achieved through the unfolding of psychological processes. That is the reason for the musically very broad, subdued setting, something which would not stand in the way of a clear understanding of the poetical argument, but would in my estimation actually enhance it. It is also the reason for the increasing rhythmic development of the melody, undisturbed by superfluous modulatory and rhythmic twists as the emotional temperature rises; for the extremely economical use of orchestral instruments in the accompaniment; and for the deliberate abstention from purely musical effects, which are only gradually introduced as the situation rises to the point at which emotion becomes more necessary than thought in grasping what is going on.'

His wife Minna's warning, after attending a rehearsal of the first production in Dresden, that the singers' contest was theatrically in danger of falling flat did not succeed in convincing Wagner that there was anything wrong with his thinking. He chose rather to blame his singers for failing to understand that, in this scene, the words were more important than the music, and with his Wolfram (Anton Mitterwurzer) he did, by dint of extra coaching, succeed in obtaining a performance that was satisfactory to him. However, singers cannot always have the benefit of the composer by their side, and there is always a danger in performance that the singers' contest is something to be borne patiently rather than enjoyed.

A similar regard for dramatic truthfulness caused Wagner to set Elisabeth's intensely introspective prayer to music of the utmost simplicity and, like the singers' contest, it brought him another warning, this time from his idol, the singer Wilhelmine Schröder-Devrient, who was to play the role of Venus. 'She sang Elisabeth's prayer to me from the piano score,' he wrote in *My Life*, 'and asked me whether I could possibly imagine that these notes could by themselves convey all that I was aiming at, when sung by a pretty young voice without a soul of its own and with none of the acuteness of a heart's essential experience. I sighed and expressed my hope that on this occasion all that was lacking would be made up for by the childlike innocence and youthfulness of this particular voice and singer.'

The singer was the composer's own niece, Johanna Wagner, who was only eighteen at the time. Despite Wilhelmine Schröder-Devrient's coaching she failed to achieve the desired effect with the prayer, and Wagner felt obliged after the first performance to make a cut in the piece. 'That on this account the most significant motivation for Elisabeth's sacrifice and death was lost,' he wrote in his guide, 'must be evident to anybody who examines the words and music closely at this point. Certainly the delivery of the whole prayer, devoid as it is of all musical figuration, demands – if it is to avoid monotony and give the impression of a deeply moving outpouring of the heart – an understanding and dedication of a kind seldom seen among the pampered opera singers of our day. A mere musical training, even of the most favoured larynx, is not enough. No device of a purely musical kind can make the delivery of this prayer interesting: only an actress who with true feminine sensitivity is able to feel within herself the unique painfulness of Elisabeth's situation – from the first suddenly awakened seed of her tenderness towards Tannhäuser, through all phases of its growth to its final blooming, redolent of death – can achieve my aim.'

Here, as in the singers' contest, we see how dangerously Wagner relied on the actors' skills, and above all on their understanding, to carry out his intentions. He went on in his guide to declare that the real triumph of a singer in the role of Elisabeth would be not only to make an effect with the whole prayer, but through her acting to prolong this effect to such an extent that the succeeding pantomime of her departure could be played in full. He added resignedly, 'I know that this is a task no less difficult than the delivery of the prayer itself, and consequently I should like to see this scene carried out in full only when the singer feels completely sure of the effect of this ceremonial dumbshow.'

Always severely self-critical, both during and after the composition of his works, Wagner believed fiercely that all he demanded of his singers and producers could be done, if only they would exert themselves to understand him. But he was sufficiently realistic, particularly in regard to his earlier works, to consent to (and even to recommend) changes and cuts rather than to see the text faithfully followed but the job badly done. His *Tannhäuser* guide is full of practical advice, even down to the manipulation of the scenery, and it also contains admissions of his own miscalculations in regard to the composition and first production of the work. From it we can get a good idea of what went wrong at the first performance and what practical steps Wagner took to repair the damage. He wrote: 'Already in the scene between Tannhäuser and Venus in the first act I found it necessary to introduce a cut for the following performances: I took out the second verse of Tannhäuser's song and Venus's preceding words. This was in no way due to any suspicion that the passage itself was dull, unpleasing or ineffective. The reason was that the whole scene came to grief in the acting, above all because it had not been possible to find a completely suitable singer for the difficult role of Venus.'

At the time of writing his guide, Wagner did not admit that the main fault might have been his own failure to provide his singer with sufficient dramatic material to bring Venus to life: he attributed his revered Wilhelmine Schröder-Devrient's inadequacy to a temperamental inability to relate to the part and explained the cut simply as an effort to save both singer and audience further embarrassment. The scene as written could – and did – make its effect, he maintained, in Liszt's later production in Weimar with a different singer. In consequence he directed that the cut he had made in Dresden should not be adopted by other producers, adding that, if the complete scene could not be done properly, he would rather see the whole production abandoned. It was only later that he brought himself to admit that the role of Venus in the Dresden version was 'all too sketchy' (as he expressed it in *My Life*), and in Paris he set about improving it, as we shall later see.

The other cut in the first act that he made in the Dresden performances was in the orchestral postlude to the finale, which was designed to express the general joy at Tannhäuser's return to the Wartburg. Since the extras who were supposed to flood on to the stage dressed as hunters at this point proved stiff and awkward, Wagner preferred to cut the postlude short, and he gave other producers, faced with a similar situation, permission to retain this cut. But he would prefer, if possible, the excitement to be brought to its highest pitch – 'to a pitch which alone enables a cheeky passage in the violins in the prelude to the second act, omitted in Dresden, to be rightly understood.'

The largest cuts of all were made in the long finale of the second act, and they included those words that Wagner described in his character study of his hero as containing the whole core of Tannhäuser's future existence: the verse beginning 'To lead the sinner to salvation'. He was himself fully aware of the damage this omission would do to his story, and he wrote in his guide: 'Unless at this moment and in this place we have absorbed the intended impression with the utmost certainty, we are no longer in a position to maintain our interest in the main figure of the drama. If we are not here at last won over to a feeling of profound sympathy for Tannhäuser, the whole course of the remaining drama becomes inconsequent and unnecessary, and all our expectations hitherto raised will remain unsatisfied. Even Tannhäuser's account in the third act of his sufferings will not be able to make up for the loss, since this account can fully make its intended effect only if it connects in our memory with this earlier and very vital impression.'

What could have possessed Wagner to have made so harmful a cut? It is a question he himself asked and answered in his guide, putting the full blame on the operatic conventions of the time. The whole company, he explained, looked on the scene simply as the customary second act ensemble, with everyone singing different words at the same time. Joseph Tichatschek, who as Tannhäuser had to voice the vital words for the first and only time, could not be persuaded to make them ring out above the surrounding jumble, and in consequence the whole adagio passage sounded monotonous and overlong, even to Wagner himself. Feeling that the scene had anyway been robbed of its significance by the way it was being done, he decided to remove the passage entirely.

He was anything but satisfied with his decision, and in his guide he pleaded with all future singers of the Tannhäuser role to lay the greatest stress on the delivery of these words. 'The cries of "*Ach, erbarm' dich mein!*" ("Have mercy on me!") demand so penetrating an accent that it is not enough to be merely a well-trained singer. The highest dramatic skill is necessary to feel the pain and despair that will give him the power to express all the horrifying depths of a grievously suffering heart: it must seem to burst forth from him like a cry for redemption.' Returning to sober practicalities, he added, 'The conductor should take care to ensure that the main singer achieves his aim successfully by utmost discretion in the accompaniment provided by the other singers as well as the orchestra.'

There was yet a further cut in the lengthy second act finale: the ensemble passage in which, after the Landgrave has ordered Tannhäuser to join the pilgrims to Rome, Elisabeth, against a background of renewed anger among the knights, prays to God to forgive him and vows to dedicate her future life to prayer. At the same time Tannhäuser is proclaiming his intention of making the pilgrimage in order to reconcile himself with his spurned angel. Though in his guide Wagner defended its dramatic aptness, he was less emphatic in his wish to see this passage restored. Indeed he wrote, 'If [in rehearsal] it does not fully succeed, that is to say, if it does not lead through the liveliness of the acting as well as the singing of the surrounding figures to an increase of the dramatic tension, or particularly if the singer of Tannhäuser should feel himself and his voice under too much of a strain after all that has gone before (especially that adagio passage with which I have just been dealing) to sing it with the necessary energy, then I myself urgently advise that the cut be retained.' He gave the same advice to Liszt in 1853, when the latter was preparing an uncut production of *Tannhäuser* in Weimar. However, he added that he would not regard any performance as satisfactory unless this passage were sung, and he left it unchanged in his Paris version.

If one detects here a hint of uncertainty, Wagner leaves us in no doubt about what should happen immediately before the curtain falls on the second act: 'The men, newly incensed by the sight of the hated adversary still amongst them, are about, with hand on sword, to turn their threats into action; an admonishing, protective gesture from Elisabeth restrains them . . . Then suddenly there comes from the valley below the sound of the young pilgrims singing, a voice of reconciliation and promise that now, while rooting the others to the spot, penetrates to Tannhäuser through the tempest of his wild remorse. Like a flash of lightning from above a ray of hope falls on his tortured feelings: tears of unutterable woe spring to his eyes, an irresistible urge brings him to cast himself at Elisabeth's feet. Not daring to raise his eyes to hers, he clutches the hem of her garment and fervently presses it to his lips. Hastily he rises, utters the cry, "To Rome!" in a tone that suggests he is entirely possessed by the suddenly awakened hope of a new life, and rushes with frantic speed from the stage. This action, to be carried out with the utmost vehemence in a very short space of time, is of the greatest significance for the final impression of the whole act; and it is this impression that is absolutely necessary to put the audience in a frame of mind that will enable the difficult third act to make its full effect.'

The action of kissing the hem of Elisabeth's garment is not described in the stage directions of the Dresden version, nor in the printed text of Wagner's *Collected Writings* (*Gesammelte Schriften und Dichtungen*), though it can be found in the stage directions of the Paris version. Clearly an afterthought, it might perhaps be regarded as a final desperate attempt to gain sympathy for Tannhäuser and to clarify the nature of his and Elisabeth's relationship to each other, so vital to Wagner's story and so damagingly obscured by cuts and tenors' whims, as well as by his own compositional miscalculations.

The revised version of the orchestral introduction to the third act, which Wagner admitted to have written originally at too great a length, was approved by the composer in his guide, with the injunction that it should not be further cut. The shortening of Elisabeth's prayer has already been dealt with, and the 'Rome Narration', that superb piece of drama with which even Tichatschek managed to win back the sympathies of his audience, plainly required no excuses. But with the concluding scene Wagner once again found himself in great difficulties. He described its original form in *My Life*: 'I had depicted Venus's new attempt to entice her faithless lover back as merely a visionary manifestation of Tannhäuser's momentary madness: only a reddish glow over the distant Hörselberg would be the outward indication of the dire situation. Likewise, the vital information of Elisabeth's death was conveyed merely through a divinatory inspiration on the part of Wolfram. The only attempt to draw the attention of the audience to the distant Wartburg was to be the scarcely audible tolling of the death bell and the scarcely discernible glow of firebrands. Right at the end the chorus of young pilgrims, to whom I had not yet given the sprouting staff, proclaimed the miracle only in words and not through any outward manifestation. This left the issue indecisive and unclear, a failing to which I had further contributed in purely musical terms by providing them with an accompaniment of lengthy and unrelieved monotony.'

By the time Wagner came to write his guide, he had already made two new versions of this final scene, the first of which was performed in Dresden in September 1846 and the second in August 1847, and he felt sufficiently confident to publish

in his score the last of these, which brings Venus back
to the stage in person and has Elisabeth's bier carried in,
accompanied by the Landgrave and his full retinue. However,
it was with some misgiving that he omitted the chorus of
the young pilgrims, finding himself forced to believe, as he
explained in his guide, that 'after what has gone before, it
could easily seem wearisome if it cannot in itself produce
a powerful effect through lavish vocal resources on the one
hand and a gripping display of acting on the other.' Only
the largest theatres would possess the means of staging the
whole final scene effectively, he observed, and only those
who could successfully extend this to include the young
pilgrims' chorus would fully satisfy him, 'since this song,
with its proclamation of the miracle, satisfactorily rounds
off the whole action, according as it does with Tannhäuser's
account of the happenings in Rome.' In a footnote in his guide
he asked interested theatres to apply directly to him for a copy
of this chorus.

The necessity to his story of this confirmation of Tannhäuser's redemption in answer to Elisabeth's prayers is so
self-evident that one can only wonder how Wagner could
ever have brought himself to omit it. And indeed there is
evidence that he felt uneasy about having done so. In 1852
he stressed to Liszt the importance of including the young
pilgrims' chorus in his Weimar production, and a year later
he wrote to Louis Schindelmeisser in Darmstadt, proposing
for the new production there an ending which sounds (apart
from Venus's appearance) very much like a reversion to the
original one: 'You will be receiving from Dresden a further
alteration to the ending of *Tannh.*: according to this revised
version, the corpse of Elisabeth does *not* appear, neither do
the Landgr. and minstrels; conversely, the younger pilgrims,
singing their chorus – as in the first revision. Conversely,

everything else – necessarily – remains, the whole of Venus's part, etc. up to "Blessed Elisabeth, pray for me", at which point the earlier ending takes over. The young pilgrims bear the blossoming staff in their midst. – Prior to that, Elisabeth's death is indicated only by the light of torches on the Wartburg, funeral bells and men's voices *coming from there* (in other words, from the top of the hill).'

He went on in his letter to give the reason for the change: 'All this talk about the appearance of a corpse, and prosaic calculations about the socio-physico-anatomical possibility of burying Elisabeth "in so short a space of time" (how fortunate that people have time on these occasions to think about time!) have finally sickened me to such an extent that I have decided on *this* alteration, or restitution.'

In thus putting the blame solely on the obtuseness of his audience Wagner signally – and uncharacteristically – failed to ask himself whether the relative ineffectiveness of this final scene might not owe something at least to the manner in which he had written both text and music, and it is even stranger that, when he came to revise his work more thoroughly in later years, he felt no urge to recast it. The essential cause of dissatisfaction is surely that so much happens within a very short space of time – Venus's attempt to regain her lover, Elisabeth's death, her funeral, Tannhäuser's death, the arrival of the pilgrims with news of the sprouting staff or the staff itself – that the audience is unable fully to absorb it all. How does Elisabeth die? Why does Tannhäuser follow suit so promptly? Is this a kind of *Liebestod*? Wagner does nothing musically – as he was later to do in *Tristan und Isolde* – to answer such questions, and nowhere is there even a fermata to help us distinguish one event from the next.

Wagner's first opportunity, since the initial performance in

Dresden, to take a direct part in the staging of *Tannhäuser* came in 1855, when he was invited by the director of the opera house in Zurich to supervise the first production of it there. Immersed at the time in the composition of *Die Walküre* and on the eve of fulfilling an engagement to conduct the Philharmonic Society's concerts in London, he only reluctantly agreed. He wrote in *My Life*: 'With these singers I went several times through their roles and in consequence found myself obliged to attend the stage rehearsals in order to keep an eye on their performances. This then meant that, pushed from one intervention to the other, I eventually reached the conductor's desk and in the end actually conducted the first performance myself. What particularly remains in my memory is the singer of Elisabeth, a former soubrette who played her role in white glacé gloves, to which a fan was attached. But by now I had had my fill of concessions and, when the audience called me on stage at the final curtain, I told my friends very plainly that this was the very last time they would get such a thing from me: I should leave it to them to do something for their own theatre, the dire state of which they had that evening been able to judge more precisely for themselves.'

It is hardly necessary to record that no new ideas arose out of that performance. The first true opportunity came four years later, when Wagner, at a loose end after completing the composition of *Tristan und Isolde*, decided to try his fortunes in Paris, where interest in his music appeared to be growing, though none of his stage works had yet been performed there. His plan was to begin with productions, under his own supervision, of his two most popular works, *Tannhäuser* and *Lohengrin*, to be followed possibly by *Tristan und Isolde*, which was due to receive its first performance in Karlsruhe early in the following year.

There is no evidence that he intended at that stage to make any alterations to *Tannhäuser*, with which the Paris season was to begin at the Théâtre Lyrique. However, two unexpected events – the cancellation of the *Tristan* première in Karlsruhe and Emperor Napoleon III's consent to the performance of *Tannhäuser* in the Opéra itself – caused him to change his plans. The resources promised him at the Opéra presented him with an opportunity not to be missed, and, with no impending production of *Tristan* to distract him, he could afford to give his whole attention to *Tannhäuser*. Though he scornfully rejected the request of the Opéra's director, Alphonse Royer, that he should write a ballet for the second act, this suggestion certainly put into his mind the idea of extending the opening scene in the Venusberg, with which he was himself dissatisfied, and thus appearing to be making some concession to Royer. He wrote to Mathilde Wesendonck on 16 April 1860: 'Venus's court was clearly the weakest part of my work. Having no good ballet in Dresden, I did what I could at that time with a few rough brush strokes, and thereby spoiled a great deal. My Venusberg was completely flat and indecisive, and as a result I lost the significant background against which the tragedy should build up. All the later memories and reminders, which should fill us with horror (because they alone explain the development of events) lost their whole effect. Anguish and tension were missing. But I realise that, at the time I wrote *Tannhäuser*, I could never have done what is called for here. It needed a much greater technical skill, which I have only now managed to acquire. Having written Isolde's final apotheosis, I can at last . . . give expression to the horror of this Venusberg.'

In his letter Wagner provided a detailed synopsis of the danced 'Bacchanale' in words almost identical to those that can now be read in the published score of the Paris *Tannhäuser*. Work on the additions to Venus's singing role progressed much more slowly, mainly because the task of securing a satisfactory text, which was being written directly in French, involved him in long hours of work with his translator (Charles Truinet), work that was furthermore constantly interrupted by discussions with officials of the Opéra on matters of casting and scenery. All this did much to dampen his original enthusiasm. He wrote to his friend Julie Ritter on 8 June 1860, 'So far I have felt insuperably indifferent to the whole affair, and the director is having some difficulty in spurring me on.' His expectation, expressed in the same letter, that he would in time rediscover his desire to work was not easily realised. There were domestic difficulties with his wife Minna, with whom he was attempting in Paris to restore their marriage. Then, after rehearsals had already begun in the Opéra, he contracted a severe fever that put him completely out of action for several weeks and left him weak and depressed. 'I have not yet managed to complete the orchestration of the new scene between Tannhäuser and Venus,' he wrote to Otto Wesendonck on 16 December 1860. 'The first scene – the dance scene – is still non-existent, and I have no idea how I shall do it.'

It was all done in the end, of course, but not in a way that suggests it was the result of any deep reappraisal of the work as a whole. The alterations that were made – extensive in the first act, minor in the second and non-existent in the third – give the impression rather of a piecemeal operation, and one that remained uncompleted for lack of time.

'The scene with Venus is the only one I shall rework entirely,' he had written to Mathilde Wesendonck in August

1860. 'The goddess of bliss will herself be touching and Tannhäuser's torment real, so that his call on the Virgin Mary will burst from his soul like a profound cry of fear.' It almost seems as if, lacking the outward tranquillity he always required for the clear functioning of his creative genius, he failed to consider whether, by making his Venus more touching (which is really to say, more human), he might stand in danger of obscuring his basic theme. In place of a man struggling to find a balance between the sensual and the spiritual sides of love within himself, we might see the drama as simply yet another version of the eternal triangle: the battle between two women for the possession of the same man. The matching remoteness of the two – the goddess of love and the pure virgin – is an essential element of the drama.

To present the goddess in a more characteristic light was a legitimate aim, and to clothe her song, *'Geliebter, komm''*, in more sensual orchestral colours, altering its former $\frac{4}{4}$ rhythm into a more pliant $\frac{3}{4}$, was a distinct gain, achieved with only a minimal rearrangement of the text. Much more questionable, however, was the decision to give Venus a second song, in which, faced with Tannhäuser's obstinate insistence on leaving her realm, she falls into a mood of self-pity. *'Ha, du kehrest nicht zurück'*, set originally to French words, is above all responsible for the reproach that the Paris version suffers from a clash of styles. It is, in its intense chromaticism, pure *Tristan und Isolde*. Whatever its intrinsic beauty, it is dramatically superfluous, since after it Venus returns to her threats against Tannhäuser, as in the Dresden score, and the scene in both versions has an identical outcome. In addition, rather than increasing our sympathetic feelings towards Tannhäuser for the 'realness' of his torment, Venus's appeal tends to make him appear singularly selfish and hard-hearted – that is to say, it produces an effect in direct opposition to that which Wagner intended.

The 'Bacchanale' itself cannot justly be reproached as out of keeping with the original style, since it is based predominantly on music already present in the Dresden score, though handled now with a virtuosity of which the younger Wagner would not have been capable. In dramatic terms that is very much in its favour, since, the aim being to provide a contrast between the unbridled sensuality of Venus's court and the timid conventionality of the Landgrave's, the wilder the display the better. Nevertheless, the extended 'Bacchanale' does present a technical problem. Since it is played immediately after the lengthy overture, the audience is confronted with a very long stretch of orchestral music before the main character of the drama is introduced and the nature of his predicament explained.

This was a problem that had troubled Wagner even in relation to the shorter Dresden version. The proper place for the overture, he wrote to his friend Theodor Uhlig in March 1852, was the concert hall, not the theatre. 'There, if the decision were left to me, I should have only the first tempo of the overture played. The remainder is too much before the drama, though otherwise too little.' And in his letter of 29 May 1852 to Liszt in connection with the Weimar production he wrote: 'Do not forget to include in your programme the explanation of the *Tannhäuser* overture I prepared for the Zurich performance of it last winter. I consider this indispensable, since it provides a condensed summary of the poetic content, though that is expressed in the overture in a way completely different from the opera itself. (In this sense you are absolutely right in seeing this overture as an entirely separate work.)'

A letter from Minna to her daughter Natalie, written on

10 February 1861, a month before the première in Paris, complained that 'Richard has cut his beautiful overture and written instead a hocus-pocus of Venus apparitions.' This suggests that Wagner did indeed consider acting on the doubts he had expressed to Uhlig and Liszt. If Minna is to be believed – and in view of her unsympathetic attitude towards the whole Paris enterprise one might legitimately suspect her of exaggeration – he would then have followed the practice he had adopted since *Lohengrin* of providing an introduction to each separate act rather than an overture to cover the whole work. In the case of *Tannhäuser* this would presumably (and logically) have been the Venusberg music. The solution he finally found was in the nature of a compromise: he retained all but the final recapitulation of the overture and composed a few bars linking it directly to the Venusberg music.

The only significant change Wagner made in the second act was a clear attempt to heighten the dramatic temperature of the singers' contest, and the fact that he made it suggests that he was no longer convinced that his attempt to write a scene in which the words were of more importance than the music had been successful. Now, immediately following Wolfram's opening exposition of the nature of love, he inserted an orchestral passage based on the Venusberg music, and with it a stage direction: 'Tannhäuser starts up as if from a dream. His defiant pose changes at once to an expression of ecstasy as he gazes into space. A slight trembling of his hand, as it involuntarily moves towards the strings of his harp, and a mysterious smile on his lips reveal that he is under a magic spell. Then, as if now waking, he firmly strikes the strings of his harp, his whole bearing suggesting that he is no longer fully aware of his surroundings, and particularly not of Elisabeth.' In this exalted state he answers Wolfram and after him Biterolf – the fourth contestant (Walther von der Vogelweide) having been eliminated, though some of his words are given to Wolfram.

The reason for the omission of Walther von der Vogelweide has become a matter for debate. In an article published in the Bayreuth Festival's *Tannhäuser* programme of 1978, tracing the alterations made by Wagner to his work at various stages of his life, Reinhard Strohm takes the traditional view that the elimination of Walther's contribution to the contest was due solely to the inability of the Paris Walther to sing it. If this were so, a simple solution would have been the one that in 1852 Wagner had offered Liszt, who was facing similar difficulties with his Walther in Weimar: this was to switch the singers of the roles of Walther (high tenor) and Heinrich der Schreiber (low tenor). However, rather than this, it seems that Wagner chose in February 1861 to rewrite Walther's song. It was set, Strohm tells us, directly to the French text and in a $\frac{3}{4}$ rhythm instead of $\frac{4}{4}$. Such an act certainly argues in favour of a desire on Wagner's part to retain Walther as a participant in the singers' contest, yet it did not prevent him finally reshaping his singers' contest in such a way that Walther takes no part in it at all, and this reshaped scene was used in the two subsequent productions of the revised *Tannhäuser* that took place in Wagner's lifetime: Hans von Bülow's in Munich and his own in Vienna. In the light of this, it seems reasonable to conclude that dramatic considerations and not mere technical problems were the true cause of Walther's disappearance. The rewritten version of his song has never been used.

A surer sense of drama also enabled Wagner at last to find a solution to the problem of bringing out that expression of Tannhäuser's contrition in the second act finale, so vital to his theme, in such a way that it would be clearly heard. The solution was so obvious that it is surprising he had not adopted it before. He wrote on 21 February 1861 to his Paris Tannhäuser, Albert Niemann: 'Only recently I came on the happy idea of leaving the ensemble out and allowing Tannhäuser to sing alone. It is the only right way.'

As it turned out, Wagner was given no chance of judging the effectiveness of these or virtually any of the other alterations he had made for the Paris production. In fact, few of them were heard at all. The overture was played in full, followed by the 'Bacchanale' (by all accounts very inadequately danced), and cuts were made in Venus's new music, since, owing to Wagner's tardiness in delivering it, the singer (Fortunata Tedesco) was unable to learn it in time. In the second act Albert Niemann refused to accept the refashioning of the singers' contest, and it was played in its original form. (How the singer of Walther von der Vogelweide fared we do not know!) Even more damaging was Niemann's refusal to sing the vital passage in the second act finale in any form, ensemble or solo, and Wagner was forced, as in Dresden, to omit it entirely.

It is scarcely surprising that his verdict on the Paris production, which he withdrew after three performances all but wrecked by hostile demonstrations, was harsh. 'All that I have now suffered was in fact no more than a just punishment for once again giving in to an illusion,' he wrote to Mathilde Wesendonck on 6 April 1861, but he added that it had not affected him very deeply: 'The performance of my work was so strange to me that what happened to it seemed no real concern of mine, and I could look on it all as just a kind of spectacle. Whether or not the affair can lead to any consequences still leaves me quite cold: all I feel in connection with it is – weariness, disgust.'

There were no consequences until some years had passed.

In the following October he wrote to his friend Wendelin Weissheimer, vaguely mentioning the possibility of staging the revised version of *Tannhäuser* in Vienna, but nothing came of that. Two years later he told Anton Pusinelli, his doctor in Dresden, that he had no intention of publishing the new scenes, and a plan he drew up for King Ludwig II of Bavaria in May 1864, envisaging a production of *Tannhäuser* in Munich in 1866 'after a partial new revision', confirms that he was not yet fully satisfied with them.

Tannhäuser in the original Dresden version was already in the repertory at Munich, and in March 1865 Wagner made use of it to demonstrate the talents of Ludwig Schnorr von Carolsfeld, his Tristan in the forthcoming first production of *Tristan und Isolde*. He described the performance in his essay 'My Memories of Ludwig Schnorr von Carolsfeld': 'With this single performance as Tannhäuser, never to be repeated, Schnorr fully realised my innermost artistic intentions: never for a moment was the daemonic element in both bliss and pain lost to view. The passage in the second act finale, "To lead the sinner to salvation . . .", the vital importance of which I had so often and so vainly stressed . . . was delivered by Schnorr, for the first and only time, with so shattering and thereby deeply moving an effect that the hero was at once transformed from an object of loathing to one deserving of the utmost pity. Through his passionate ravings of remorse during the violently animated finale of the second act and his equally emotional parting from Elisabeth, his appearance as a madman in the third act was properly motivated, and all the more gripping in consequence was the transition from numbness to feeling, until the renewed attack of madness precipitated the magical reappearance of Venus with almost as much daemonic force as, in the first act, the cry to the Virgin Mary had miraculously restored the everyday Christian world. In his final ravings of despair Schnorr was truly awe-inspiring, and I cannot believe that either Kean or Ludwig Devrient as Lear could have achieved a more powerful effect.'

However, Wagner's own satisfaction with the performance was not shared by all members of the audience: 'Much of it, such as the all but wordless scene after the magical release from the Venusberg, proved properly gripping and led to stormy outbreaks of undivided public approval. On the whole, however, I detected more in the way of surprise and amazement. Particularly all that was new to the audience, such as the otherwise invariably omitted passage in the second act finale, produced, through its divergence from the familiar, an almost alienating effect. I was then obliged to be put right by a friend, not otherwise lacking in intelligence, who told me straight out that I really had no right to wish *Tannhäuser* done in my own particular way, since the public as well as my friends, who had everywhere given this work a favourable reception, had clearly indicated thereby that the former more congenial, less colourful version was basically the more correct one, however dissatisfied I myself might be with it. My protest over the stupidity of such assertions was dismissed with a friendly and compassionate shrug of the shoulders.'

Wagner's lofty dismissal of his friend's advice as being nothing more than evidence of 'the very widespread laxity, not to say depravity' of modern public taste may have served – together with the proof Schnorr had given him that with conscientious application *Tannhäuser* could be made to work very well as he had originally written it – to persuade him that for the moment he would be better employed completing a new work than tampering any further with an old one. When the time came, in the summer of 1867, to stage the promised new version of *Tannhäuser* in Munich, he had done no further work on it. Now settled in Tribschen and busy orchestrating *Die Meistersinger*, he was also disillusioned with King Ludwig. The king had offended him by dismissing Tichatschek, whom Wagner had invited to Munich to demonstrate how the role of Lohengrin could and should be sung, and Wagner was in no mood to respond to Ludwig's request that he should return to Munich to supervise the new production of *Tannhäuser*. He had reached the bitter conclusion that, when it came to the test, Ludwig was proving just as capricious as all the other princes who had let him down in the past. He wrote to the king on 25 June 1867: 'Believe me, nothing can be achieved here by issuing orders: in my excellent [Hans von] Bülow you now have a conductor who will see to it better than any other that the music is properly played, and with that you will have to rest content. Anything else would be a hollow mockery.'

True to his word, he took no part in the production, and neither he nor the king was present at the first performance on 1 August. According to Strohm some, though not all, of the alterations Wagner had made for Paris were observed. The reshaped singers' contest was used for the first time, but the overture was played in full in spite of Wagner's instructions to the contrary.

The next opportunity to come to grips with the work was thrust on Wagner rather than sought. The invitation came in 1875 from the director of the Vienna Opera, Franz Jauner, who had proved accommodating in allowing some of his singers to take part in rehearsals of the *Ring* in Bayreuth

that summer. For fear of jeopardising their friendly relations Wagner agreed to supervise new productions of both
Tannhäuser and *Lohengrin* in Vienna. Though other opera
houses were still, with Wagner's acquiescence, bringing out
new productions of the Dresden *Tannhäuser*, Jauner insisted
on having the revised version. No doubt Wagner saw the
advantage to himself of gauging the effect of all the changes
he had made but not yet seen on stage. However, physically
weary after the strenuous rehearsals of the *Ring* in the summer, and mentally preoccupied with the launching of the
first Bayreuth festival in the coming year, he was not in the
right frame of mind to reimmerse himself in *Tannhäuser*. In
addition to that (or perhaps because of it) he was content with
neither cast, nor scenery nor orchestra, which was conducted
by Hans Richter.

His production made use of all the new material he had
written for Paris, including the reshaped singers' contest,
and, for the first time on any stage, the truncated overture
leading straight into the Venusberg music was used. But,
if he had further changes in mind (as his 1864 plan for a
model production in Munich suggests), he did not choose to
make them in Vienna. His single additional change, as Strohm
records, was a shortening of the note value of the word '*aller*'
in the young pilgrims' chorus at the end of the opera, an
alteration so tiny that it was overlooked when the score
eventually came to be published. And Jauner, after Wagner
had left Vienna vowing never to return, immediately restored
the overture to its full length.

Such was Wagner's final attempt to solve the problems of
Tannhäuser on the stage. There still remained the problem of
publication. Never the most clear-sighted of businessmen,
he had got himself into a particular muddle with his previous publishers (Fürstner in Berlin and Flaxland in Paris),

and his attempt to persuade Schott to acquire all the rights from them failed to materialise. In his letter to Schott he expressed his intention, once *Tannhäuser* was published in its revised form, of insisting that theatres should use this and no previous edition. However, no such edition appeared in Wagner's lifetime, and thus we have been left forever in doubt regarding the form his own 'final version' might have taken.

As his remarks quoted at the beginning of this chapter show, Wagner had serious misgivings about the dramatic validity of his rewritten Venusberg scene. That Cosima retained it in her own production at Bayreuth in 1891 might owe more to her avowed personal preference for it than to a pious respect for the composer's expressed wishes. Her example has not been generally followed: the original Dresden version has continued to lead a vigorous life in theatres throughout the world. Indeed, Bayreuth itself eventually capitulated. Wieland Wagner's first production of *Tannhäuser* at the festival theatre in 1954 was a blend of all the existing versions. Violently attacked as it was by traditionalists (however shaky the ground on which they stood), it remains in my experience the most successful attempt to provide a balance between the deficiencies of the original score and the excesses of the revised version without interfering with the musical substance of either.

Of course it was not a 'final version' and made no claims to be, Wieland Wagner modestly presenting it as 'a subject for discussion'. But, based as it was on a close study of all the written sources, it pointed firmly in the right direction. What Wagner set out to express in *Tannhäuser* can be found clearly defined in the text, in the stage directions, in 'A Communication to my Friends', in his autobiography, and above all in his guide to producers, 'On the Performing of

Tannhäuser', which, though written before the Paris version came into existence, provides an illuminating vision of the goal towards which every production, whether based on the Dresden or the Paris version or a combination of both, should aim. If only more producers would read it!

My Final Victory over Life:

The Evolution of *Parsifal*

In April 1857 Wagner, then working on *Siegfried*, moved into the Asyl, the little house which his benefactors, Otto and Mathilde Wesendonck, had had built for him in the grounds of their villa on the outskirts of Zurich. He wrote about it in his autobiography *My Life*: 'On Good Friday I awoke for the first time in this house. The sun was shining, the little garden was clothed in green, birds were singing, and eventually I was able to seat myself down on the cottage balcony to enjoy the peace for which I had so long been yearning. As I was basking in this, it suddenly came into my mind that today was Good Friday, and I recalled the deep impression this admonition had once made on me while reading Wolfram's *Parzival*. Since those days in Marienbad, when I conceived both *Die Meistersinger* and *Lohengrin*, I had never given any further thought to that poem. Now the idea contained in it took such overwhelming possession of me that, beginning with the Good Friday concept, I quickly conceived a complete drama, which I at once sketched out, divided into three acts, in a few fleeting strokes.'

Later Wagner told his wife Cosima that he had made a mistake in his autobiography. It had not been on Good Friday that those feelings came to him: rather it was the peacefulness of the Asyl garden that had brought back to him the mood of Good Friday. The mistake is of no consequence: the important point is that the Good Friday concept – the idea of redemption and reconciliation – formed from the very start the central theme of the drama which, though the seed had been planted in 1845, when he was only thirty-two (his age at the time he read Wolfram von Eschenbach's epic poem in Marienbad), was not to come to fruition until the very end of his life.

This was no accident, nor was it the result of those disruptions in his life that held up the completion of both the *Ring* and *Die Meistersinger* for so many years. Wagner often said that *Parsifal* would be his final work, his last message to erring humanity, and he felt instinctively that he would not be able to write it until he himself had attained the right state of mind, a mood of detachment from the cares of the world and of resignation in the Schopenhauerian sense of the word.

When at last, at the age of sixty-four, he felt able to embark on *Parsifal*, it was not, as Nietzsche uncharitably maintained, a case of 'old Romanticists who one day fall on their faces and lie, one knows not why, stretched out at the foot of the Cross,' but rather a final statement of views he had held all his life. They were certainly not purely Christian views, nor were they exclusively religious, but they had very much to do with the moral problems that underlie all Wagner's works. One of these, which found early expression in the character of Senta in *Der Fliegende Holländer* and which dominates the story of *Parsifal*, is fellow-feeling. As Wagner himself declared, 'It is this fellow-feeling that I recognise as the strongest feature of my moral nature, and presumably it is also the fount of my art.'

This sentence was written on 1 October 1858 in a diary that Wagner, after leaving the Asyl, wrote in Venice for Mathilde Wesendonck's benefit, and it was occasioned by what might be regarded by many as a very trivial event: the sight of a chicken being slaughtered in a poultry dealer's shop. Wagner did not regard it as trivial. 'The bird's dreadful scream and the mournful weakening squawks as it was overpowered filled my whole soul with horror,' he observed. 'I have never been able to rid myself of this impression, however often experienced before and since. It is horrible to think on what a bottomless pit of misery of the cruellest sort our basically pleasure-seeking existence depends.'

He went on to say that he found it hard to feel sympathy with human beings, particularly rich ones, since all their efforts seemed to be directed towards shutting out feelings of compassion in order to preserve their own peace of mind. His pity was directed more towards animals: 'These I see as completely excluded from the ability to raise themselves above suffering, from resignation and from the profound, divine comfort that this resignation provides. When they come to know suffering, as occurs when they are tortured like this, all I see and feel in my own heart, with agonised despair, is absolute suffering, without hope of redemption, without any sense of a higher purpose. The only release from it is death, thus reinforcing the feeling that it would have been better had the creature never been born. If there is any point in this suffering, it can only be its ability to arouse a sense of fellow-feeling in a human being, who thereby absorbs within himself the animal's fruitless existence and, by recognising the vanity of all existence, becomes the world's saviour. (This interpretation will one day become clear to you in the third act of *Parzival*, which takes place on the morning of Good Friday.) To see this human capacity to save the world through compassion go to seed, undeveloped and indeed quite wilfully neglected – this is what makes individual human beings so repugnant to me and reduces my compassion for them to the point of complete indifference to their distress. Redemption offers to every human being in distress a way out that is closed to all animals. The more he fails to see this, or indeed strives to keep it out of sight, the more strongly do I feel the urge to fling these doors wide open to him, and I can go to truly brutal lengths to make him aware of the misery of suffering.'

There had always been in Wagner, as this passage suggests, a longing for peace and harmony, and, if the outward circumstances of his life prevented him from attaining them personally – how much his own behaviour contributed to that failure is of course a different question – that remained the final goal. His works up to this time had all reflected this longing, but in each of them human fallibility had brought their participants to grief before the goal was attained. Redemption, Wagner seemed to be telling us, was attainable only after death, not in life. In the figure of Parzival, that legendary knight of King Arthur's court, whose distress lay in his frustrated ability to do good to others, he saw a hero through whom the goal could be shown as attainable in a living world. So vivid, in fact, was this figure in his imagination during this time in Venice when he was writing *Tristan und Isolde* that he even contemplated bringing Parzival to visit the wounded Tristan in the third act, an idea he eventually abandoned as an unnecessary divergence.

But the connection in his mind between the two dramas, the one he was then working on and the other which was still floating in his imagination, remained overwhelming. He wrote to Mathilde from Lucerne on 29 May 1859, while still at work on *Tristan*: 'This final act has all the characteristics of a true intermittent fever: the deepest, unparalleled suffering and yearning, turning abruptly to unparalleled cheering and rejoicing . . . This has once more changed my feelings towards *Parzival*. It has recently become clear to me again that this too will be a very difficult piece of work. Strictly speaking, the principal and central figure is Anfortas. That suddenly became terribly clear to me: he is my third-act Tristan raised to unimaginable heights. His spear wound, and yet another wound on top of that: in his heart the poor man in his frightful agony has no other longing but to die. His constant craving, in order to win this solace, is for a sight of the Grail, in the hope that this will at least heal his wounds, nothing else having proved capable of it. Nothing can help him, nothing. All the Grail can bring him, however, is the single, invariable message – that he *cannot* die. In fact, the sight of it only increases his torments by conferring immortality on them.'

At this period Wagner was still using the names of the characters (Parzival, Anfortas) as they appear in Wolfram von Eschenbach's poem, and he was only gradually bringing the crowded events of that huge and diffuse epic into a condensed dramatic form. In Wolfram the kingdom of the Grail, Monsalvat, is a semi-fabulous territory that has no clear geographical position, but becomes visible only to those who have the right to enter it. Parzival, the ignorant young knight who stumbles on it apparently by chance, has this right because, though he does not know it, his mother Herzeleide is the sister of Anfortas, the present Grail king, and he is consequently the rightful heir. He is ejected from Monsalvat because, on seeing the wounded Anfortas for the first time, he fails to ask the cause of the wound, a question that would have had the effect of healing the king.

As this episode reveals, the fairy-tale element is strong in Wolfram, and indeed much is left unexplained. Here the Grail is simply a magic stone with the capacity of providing food and prolonging life, and the spear is just an item in the ceremonial equipment of the knights of the Grail, not the weapon that wounded Anfortas.

Parzival's bewilderment at being ejected from Monsalvat

turns to resentment when the Grail's messenger, a witchlike woman called Condrie, denounces him before King Arthur's assembled court for having failed to put the question that would have saved Anfortas. Understandably, he cannot see why an alleged sin, committed in ignorance, should be held against him, and he rejects a God who, though supposedly omnipotent, can allow such injustice. He spends several adventurous years in trying to recover his knightly honour, but it is only a chance meeting on a Good Friday with a hermit that finally leads to his reconciliation with God. The hermit, Trevrizent, is Anfortas's brother, and therefore Parzival's uncle. Shortly after this encounter, Condrie arrives at King Arthur's court. She begs Parzival's forgiveness for her previous denunciation of him and tells him that he has been proclaimed king of the Grail (the consequence, it should be pointed out, not of his chivalrous deeds, but of his blood relationship with Anfortas). Parzival returns with Condrie to Monsalvat, where he now puts the question that he had failed to ask earlier. Since he has already been proclaimed king, this is little more than a formality, but it does have the effect of curing Anfortas. Parzival is then joined at Monsalvat by the wife he has acquired in the meantime, Condwiramurs, and their children, among them Lohengrin.

It is clear from this brief summary why Wagner later vigorously denied that his *Parsifal* was an adaptation of Wolfram's epic. He was in fact severely critical of Wolfram, who, he told Mathilde in his letter of 29 May 1859, had not understood the true significance of the things he was writing about. 'He strings event to event, adventure to adventure, uses the Grail motive to provide strange and curious procedures and images, gropes around and leaves the awed reader wondering exactly what he is trying to say. Whereupon all he can reply is: I don't really understand it, any more than a holy priest understands his Christianity when he acts it out in front of his altar.'

Not Wolfram, but an old French legend, which he does not further identify, gave Wagner the idea of turning the Grail into the drinking cup of the Last Supper, in which Joseph of Arimathaea caught the blood of Christ on the Cross. Wagner continued in his letter: 'What a terrible significance Anfortas's relationship with this miraculous chalice hereby gains! He, afflicted with the same wound, dealt him by a rival's spear in the course of a passionate love escapade – he must yearn, as his only solace, for the blessing of the blood that once, from a similar wound, flowed from the side of the Saviour as He languished, world-renouncing, world-redeeming, world-suffering, on the Cross. Blood for blood, wound for wound, but between blood and wound, then and now, what a huge gulf!'

With one dramatic point now established, Wagner was still faced with many other problems, particularly in regard to the hero himself: 'What a lot I should have to do with Parzival, for Wolfram understands absolutely nothing about him either: his despair over God is stupid and unmotivated, his conversion even less adequate. That matter of the "question" is in the worst possible taste and completely meaningless. Here I may have to rely entirely on my own invention. And there is yet another difficulty to face in regard to Parzival. He is utterly indispensable as the saviour Anfortas in longing for; yet, if Anfortas is to be shown in the light fully worthy of him, he will be of such immense tragic interest that it will be next door to impossible to set up a second main point of interest against him. Yet this main point of interest must be directed towards Parzival if he is not just to appear at the end as a *deus ex machina*, leaving one completely cold. So Parzival's development, his sublime purification, though preordained by his whole thoughtful, deeply compassionate nature, must be brought to the foreground. And for that I cannot make use of the broad layout that Wolfram had at his disposal: I must condense everything into *three* main situations, each so drastic in its import that the profound, ramified content comes clearly and sharply into view; for to fashion and depict things in this way is the basis of all my art. And I am supposed to tackle another such task? God preserve me from it! Today I bid farewell to this senseless project: Geibel can do it, and Liszt set it to music. When my old friend Brünnhilde springs into the funeral pile, I shall hurl myself after her and hope for a blissful end. May that be my final word – amen!'

Yet in spite of his avowals the subject continued to develop inside him. From Paris, where he went after the completion of *Tristan und Isolde* to present *Tannhäuser*, he wrote to Mathilde at the beginning of August 1860: 'Parzival is very much in my mind again. It is all becoming increasingly clear to me, and when everything is fully ripened inside me, the completion of this work should afford me the greatest enjoyment. But it will take a good few years yet. And this time I should also like to leave it to words alone. I shall hold it at arm's length as long as I can, and occupy myself with it only when it takes me by force. Then this wonderful process of creation will make me forget all my miseries. Shall I chatter on about it? Have I already told you that the fabulously wild messenger of the Grail is to be at one and the same time the seductive woman of the second act? Since this occurred to me, practically everything in the story has become clear in my mind. This curiously repellent creature who slavishly serves the knights of the Grail with tireless diligence, who carries out impossible missions, who lies in a corner, just waiting until she is given something unheard-of and onerous to do – this creature vanishes entirely now and again, how and whither no one knows. Then suddenly one encounters her again, terribly exhausted, pale, wretched and repulsive, yet once again, tireless as a dog, serving the Grail, though showing signs of a secret contempt for its knights. Her eyes seem always to be seeking the right one, whom after previous mistakes she has still to find. But what she is seeking she does not really know: it is all just instinct.'

The fusion of the Grail's messenger with the seductress of Act Two greatly strengthened Wagner's dramatic plan by integrating Klingsor as well as Condrie into the action. In Wolfram both are peripheral figures, and there is no connection between them. Nor indeed is there any connection between Klingsor and the knights of the Grail. Wolfram's Klingsor is merely a cruel magician who holds a large number of women captive, and it is not even Parzival who defeats him, but Gawain. The idea of Klingsor as a hermit seeking to become a knight of the Grail and bent on revenge for his rejection by Titurel is Wagner's own.

Certainly Condrie (or Kundry, as Wagner eventually named her) is an enigmatic figure in Wolfram as in Wagner. She is a hideously ugly woman who dresses in elegant clothing (a hint of her noble birth) and rides around on a donkey. However, her mystery is peculiar to herself: basically it has nothing to do with Parzival's mission. Wagner, by identifying her with the seductress of his second act, not only brought her effectively into the central action: he also in the process provided himself with a new mystical dimension – that of reincarnation.

He had become fascinated with this religious belief when planning his Buddhist drama *Die Sieger*, and his letter from Paris to Mathilde Wesendonck reveals how deeply it had stirred his imagination. Before writing the letter he had been rereading *Lohengrin* with a view to a French publication of the text: 'I cannot avoid regarding this poem as the most tragic of all, since true reconciliation can only be found by casting an awesomely farseeing eye over the world. Only a deeply considered acceptance of the idea of reincarnation could reveal to me the consoling point at which everything at last comes together on the same level of redemption, when various lives, running separately side by side within the framework of time, converge sympathetically outside of time. According to the beautiful Buddhist belief, Lohengrin's flawless purity is explained by the fact that he is the continuation of Parzival, who had to struggle to attain that purity. In the same way, Elsa would attain the level of Lohengrin in her reincarnation. And so my plan for *Die Sieger* has come to look to me like the concluding sequel of *Lohengrin*. All the terrible tragedy of life would be seen to lie solely in the division between time and space: but, since time and space are only *our* way of looking at things, having no real existence beyond that, even sufferings of the most tragic kind must be seen by the enlightened person as attributable solely to individual error. I believe that is how it is.'

Though it originated in connection with *Die Sieger*, the concept of 'time and space' ('*Zeit und Raum*') was to find its expression in *Parsifal* in the transformation scene of the first act:

'PARSIFAL: I scarcely move my feet, yet seem to have travelled far.

GURNEMANZ: You see, my son, here time and space are one.'

It is remarkable how long these two works ran simultaneously but separately in Wagner's mind without his consciously realising to what extent they were two aspects of the same drama, one in which the idea of reincarnation played a central part. Wagner's Kundry, the seductress of Amfortas, is the reincarnation of all sinning womanhood ('*Höllenrose*', Klingsor calls her, 'Herodias' and 'Gundrygia'). Between her

and Amfortas stands the innocent Parsifal, to whom with
fine dramatic irony Wagner makes both look for redemption,
without really knowing why. Amfortas, awaiting the 'pure
fool' whose coming, he has been told, will cure his wound,
fails to recognise his saviour when he first arrives; Kundry,
only dimly conscious of previous sinful existences while she
is the Grail's messenger, knows the reason for the curse under
which she lies only when she is the seductress in Klingsor's
power.

True to his prediction in his letter to Mathilde Wesendonck,
Parsifal took many years to ripen in Wagner's mind, but in
a letter to King Ludwig II of Bavaria, written on Good
Friday 1865 (14 April) while he was busy preparing the
first production of *Tristan und Isolde* in Munich, Wagner
revealed that it was still very much in his thoughts: 'A
warm and sunny Good Friday once gave me, through its
mood of blessedness, the idea of *Parzival*. Since then it has
lived inside me, growing like a child in its mother's womb.
On each Good Friday it becomes a year older, and I then
celebrate the day of its conception, to be followed one day
by its birth.'

He went on to relate how, on Good Friday of the previous
year, he had passed through Munich (this, though he did
not say so, was while he was fleeing to Switzerland from
his creditors in Vienna). There in a shop window he saw
a portrait of the young prince who had just ascended the
throne: 'Sad as I was, I nevertheless celebrated on this Good
Friday the conception of my *Parzival* – indeed, the picture
in that little back street had involuntarily led me back to my
hero: the young king and Parzival dissolved into one . . .
Grey and cold outside, no hope within, tired and longing
for death, what did I not dream of on that last Good Friday
here in Munich – close to the highest glory of my life, to

the sun that was to illumine my night, to my redeemer, the saviour of my life! It is – a wonder, for it is more wonderful than anything a poet can invent . . . Now the birth of *Tristan* is approaching; it grows, it flourishes: each day brings us a celebration, a thanksgiving festival for King Parzival!'

This can, of course, be dismissed by the uncharitable as mere sycophantic flattery, but there had indeed arisen in Wagner's mind the feeling of a mystical connection between the young king and the hero of his still unwritten work. Following the production of *Tristan* Wagner went off, in August 1865, to Ludwig's hunting lodge on the Hochkopf with the intention of completing the orchestration of the second act of *Siegfried*. As reading material he took with him a German translation of the Sanskrit epic *Ramayana*. That poem might have been the direct cause of his decision to put off work on *Siegfried* in favour of sketching out a scenario for *Parzival*, yet it struck Wagner as more than a coincidence, rather a mysterious meeting of minds, that, at the very moment of starting work on it, he received a letter from the king pleading for that very thing. Across a full page of his *Brown Book* (*Braunes Buch*), in which he was about to begin his scenario, he wrote, 'How strange! The king is ardently demanding to hear about Parzival.'

The scenario, some seven thousand words long, shows how greatly the subject had now matured in his mind. Written in narrative form with no direct indications of the work's future dramatic shape, it falls naturally into a series of 'main situations', the invention of which, as Wagner had previously told Mathilde Wesendonck, was an essential part of his artistic method. Except for a few points of detail, the sketch contains the whole essence of the drama as it finally emerged, as well as several fragments of dialogue which were eventually taken over almost intact. The most significant addition to the story as outlined to Mathilde was the figure of Gurnemans (as he was named in the scenario), an elderly knight of the Grail who had served under the previous king, Titurel, and taken part in the fight with Klingsor in which Anfortas was wounded. Through Gurnemans Wagner was now able to describe the events preceding the story's opening, and thereafter to make use of him as guide and tutor to the young and foolish Parzival, who was brought on the scene with an action that originated entirely in Wagner's own imagination: the killing of the swan.

In Wolfram's epic Gurnemans is simply an elderly knight who takes a fatherly interest in the young Parzival and instructs him in knightly behaviour: he has nothing at all to do with Monsalvat and the Grail. In his sketch Wagner turned him into Titurel's former squire, a kindly, but somewhat rough character strongly reminiscent of Tristan's Kurwenal. His development into the gentle philosopher of the finished work occurred later. However, in either form his invention provided Wagner with the solution to his main problem: how to place Parzival, rather than Anfortas, in the forefront of his drama. Gurnemans is the still centre around whom the three main protagonists, Parzival, Anfortas and Kundry, revolve, and it is through him that their unrecognised relationships with one another are reflected.

The one dramatic problem still to be resolved concerned the holy spear, which by now had been identified by Wagner as the weapon with which the soldier Longinus pierced Christ's side on the Cross. In Wolfram's epic the spear with which Anfortas was wounded was in the keeping of the knights of the Grail, and thus Wagner had it in the first pages of his sketch. He was then struck by the inconsequentiality of Wolfram's account, and he decided to place the spear in Klingsor's possession. It then became the weapon with which

Klingsor subsequently tried to destroy Parzival, and which Parzival caught and used to destroy Klingsor. However, Wagner was still not clear by what means Klingsor had come to possess the spear. Two days after finishing his scenario and despatching it to the king, he wrote down in his *Braunes Buch* two possible solutions. The first was that Anfortas took the spear with him when he set out to defeat Klingsor, and Klingsor snatched it and wounded him with it while he was otherwise engaged with Kundry. The second was that the knights of the Grail had in fact never possessed the spear and were troubled by the knowledge that, until they discovered it, their power would not be complete. Klingsor knew this too and, having in some way gained possession of it himself, he was determined to keep it. The resemblance of this version to Wotan's dilemma with the Nibelung's ring is obvious, and that is probably why Wagner eventually rejected it in favour of the first alternative. But it is remarkable that so integral a part of the dramatic action – indeed the very point on which it all depends – should have been in the nature of an afterthought rather than the initial spur to Wagner's imagination.

King Ludwig, when he read the *Parzival* sketch, was puzzled, however, by something else. 'Why is our hero converted only by Kundry's kiss?' he asked. 'Why is it *that* that makes his divine mission clear to him?' Wagner replied: 'That is an awesome secret, my dear friend! You remember, of course, the serpent in Paradise and its tempting promise. Adam and Eve became "knowing", they became "conscious of sin". For this consciousness the human race had to atone in misery and shame until redeemed by Christ, who took the sins of mankind on himself. My friend, can I speak of such serious matters other than in parables, through metaphors? Only the enlightened can grasp the inner meaning for himself.

Adam and Eve: Jesus Christ. How would it be to place beside them Anfortas and Kundry: Parzival? But with great caution! The kiss that leads to Anfortas's downfall arouses in Parzival a complete awareness of that sin – not, however, his own sin, but that of the pitiful sufferer, whose laments he had previously only dully heard, but the cause of which now becomes clear to him through his own sinful fellow-feeling. Now he knows more than all the others, and particularly more than the knights of the Grail, who had always believed Anfortas was complaining simply on account of his spear wound. Parzival now sees more deeply.'

Between the writing of this scenario and the next assumption of serious work on *Parsifal* ten years elapsed, the years in which Wagner completed both *Die Meistersinger* and the *Ring* and built his own theatre in Bayreuth. During this immensely busy period, however, *Parsifal* was not completely forgotten. Cosima Wagner's diaries reveal how often it was the subject of conversation in Tribschen and Wahnfried, and occasionally the prose sketch of 1865 was brought out and read to friends, among them Nietzsche. Wagner's urge to get seriously down to work on it did in fact precede the first production of the *Ring* in the summer of 1876, but all the activities connected with that event prevented him from doing more than reading books in order to re-immerse himself in the atmosphere of the Holy Grail.

Cosima mentions some of these in her diaries. They include August Friedrich Gfrörer's *History of Early Christianity* (*Geschichte des Urchristentums*), Joseph Görres's *Christian Mysticism* (*Die christliche Mystik*), an essay by Friedrich Theodor Vischer on David Strauss's book *The Old and New Faith* (*Der alte und der neue Glaube*), San Marte's *Parzival Studies* (*Parzival-Studien*) and the collection of Sanskrit fables entitled *Pancha tantra*. Wagner also reread Wolfram von Eschenbach's

Parzival. He had already expressed, as mentioned earlier, his dissatisfaction with that work to Mathilde Wesendonck. Wolfram, he felt, was too much a child of his own medieval times – 'his barbaric, totally confused century, hovering between early Christianity and the more modern political economy', as he put it – to perceive the deeper implications of his story, and all he had done was 'to take his material from the bad French chivalric romances of his time and chatter on like a starling in their style.'

Wagner had already depicted the medieval attitude towards religion in his drama about Parzival's son Lohengrin. Now, in dealing with Parzival himself, he was seeking a less historical approach, one in which, as in *Tristan* and the *Ring*, the emphasis lay on the eternal, rather than the temporal verities. Always the enemy of church dogma, Protestant as well as Catholic, he looked on the Gospels as repositories of ancient legends rather than as accounts of actual happenings. In this respect he was just as much a child of his own time as Wolfram, for the spirit of rationalism was strong in the nineteenth century, and Wagner was an admirer of Ernest Renan's controversial *History of the Origins of Christianity*, as also of Charles Darwin's *The Origin of Species*. However, this did not lessen his veneration of Jesus Christ, as an entry on 12 May 1879 in Cosima's diaries shows: 'He has come to see clearly that it is Christ's sinlessness which distinguishes him from all others and makes him so moving in his mercy. All the other founders of religions and saints, like Buddha, for example, started as sinners and became saints, but Christ could not commit a sin.' His recognition of Christ's sinlessness, which, as he put it, was 'predestined in his mother's womb', was the starting point of his religious outlook. As he told Cosima on another occasion, 'I cannot be sinless like Jesus, but I can revere sinlessness, and seek pardon from my ideal when I am unfaithful to it.'

Such was the figure Wagner set out to represent in Parsifal, who was certainly not free of sin, even if he did resist the temptations of unchastity. And for this reason he always indignantly repudiated assertions by both disciples and opponents that Parsifal was a reflection of Jesus Christ. He was at most a saint, he claimed, one of those human beings whom he admired more for their steadfastness and singlemindedness than for the purity of their religious faith. His own faith, as we have seen, was anything but pure, when viewed from an orthodox Christian angle. He regarded the Gospels, as he regarded the Sanskrit legends of the *Pancha tantra*, from a philosophical angle, and used symbolic episodes from them in the same way that he had used symbolic episodes from the Nordic sagas in the *Ring*, that is to say, as graphic illustrations of his chosen theme. The most striking examples in *Parsifal* are the representation of the Last Supper, and Kundry's ceremony in the third act of anointing Parsifal's feet and drying them with her own hair. In making use of such episodes, Wagner perhaps failed to consider sufficiently the particular values these Christian symbols had acquired in the Western world, where in the minds of his audience they were identified with doctrine rather than legend. This was to lead to misunderstandings of a kind he had already experienced with *Tannhäuser*. In that work Tannhäuser's pilgrimage to Rome and the breaking into leaf of the Pope's staff were interpreted by many people as evidence of his Catholic outlook. A Protestant and avowed anti-Catholic, Wagner had been irritated, but he succeeded in persuading himself that the misunderstanding was due to the obtuseness of his fellow mortals rather than to a misjudgement of his own, and in *Parsifal* he deliberately took a similar risk again. He knew, he told Cosima, that he was living in a world that had little feeling for myth, but he always cherished the hope that one day he would be understood.

In his correspondence with Mathilde Wesendonck nearly twenty years earlier Wagner had written of his intention of making Parzival the subject of a spoken rather than a music drama. That idea was soon dropped, and in all subsequent references to the work he left no doubt that he saw it as a music drama. It seems, however, that he conceived no musical ideas for it until 1876, when, while improvising themes for the march that had been commissioned by Philadelphia to celebrate the centenary of the American Declaration of Independence, he chanced on a melody which, he told Cosima on 16 February 1876, would be 'the chorus the women will sing to Parzival: "*Komm, schöner Knabe!*"'. It is hardly necessary to say that he did not use it in the *Philadelphia March*.

His resolve to settle down to continuous work was made in January 1877. He began writing the text at once, starting with a prose sketch in dialogue form, and within a week he was able to tell Cosima that he had solved the last dramatic problem: the loss of the spear to Klingsor and its recovery would now be at the centre of the action. He achieved this by making the knights of the Grail aware that only the recovery of the spear can heal the king's wound. 'I shamefully lost it,' Anfortas says on his very first appearance in the first act. 'All who have braved that magic power in an attempt to recover it have perished. No one will recover it except the one whom the Grail has chosen: the knowing fool – and who can find him?' As if to make sure the audience will absorb this, Wagner made Gurnemanz (now spelt thus) repeat it to the young squires immediately before Parzival's entrance. In case even this was not enough, Wagner gave to the unseen boys' voices in the temple these words to sing: 'Have faith in the spear when, in compassionate suffering, a knowing fool shall regain it.' Parzival, in this version, is the only person who is ignorant of the healing power of the spear, until, as if by intuition, he seizes it as Klingsor aims it at him at the end of the second act.

By the end of February the prose sketch was completed, and Wagner then began turning it into verse, a task that occupied him no more than six weeks. In the course of this work, or even later, while engaged on the music, he removed the direct references to the spear. Perhaps he felt them to be too explicit. However, he retained the general outline of the idea, entrusting it to the orchestra to indicate the dramatic significance of the spear by his use of the motive associated with it at all relevant points.

The flavour of the melody that had come to him while working on the *Philadelphia March* induced Wagner to change the nature of Klingsor's maidens. In the 1865 scenario they had been described as 'she-devils': now they became what he described to Cosima as 'languishing' figures. It was a fruitful change, for it introduced into the drama a new psychological concept, more subtle than the original contrast between the 'good' knights of the Grail and the 'wicked' maidens. It was the idea of the essential innocence of Nature, represented by the Flower Maidens, and it gave an extra profundity to the conciliatory message of the Good Friday scene.

The alteration of the hero's name from Parzival to Parsifal was based on something Wagner had read in Joseph Görres's *Christian Mysticism*. From this he gathered that in Arabic the word 'parsi' meant 'pure', and the word 'fal' meant 'fool'. Görres's etymology is regarded by the experts as highly dubious, but in the final result that is of little significance, for it provided Wagner with a wonderful opportunity to bring his hero and Kundry together in the second act, when he hears her call his forgotten name in Klingsor's Magic Garden. At the same time, it reminds the audience of the significance of the 'pure fool' in the drama as a whole. Kundry can now tell Parsifal (and the audience) of his childhood and his mother's death and offer herself to him in consolation: all this achieved, through the explanation of his name, in a wholly spontaneous manner.

The last important difference between the 1865 scenario and the rhymed text comes at the end of the drama. In the scenario Wagner allowed Parzival, after curing Anfortas by touching his thigh with the holy spear, to describe in detail the reasons for all his sufferings. In the final text this is all simplified: Parsifal does not spend time in pointing out to Amfortas (as he is now named) the moral of the story, which suggests that Wagner had in the meantime learnt a lesson from composing *Götterdämmerung*, where he had cut out a similar lecture from Brünnhilde. The music, he had realised then and realised again now, could express the moral more profoundly than any words. So Parsifal takes over his kingly duties with only the briefest of explanations and presides over the Grail ceremony himself, without waiting for Amfortas's invitation.

Wagner began work on the music immediately on his return from the 'cure' in Bad Ems that followed his conducting engagement in London. Cosima, who arrived back in Bayreuth two days after her husband, noted in her diary on 11 August 1877: 'Many affectionate outpourings and finally the revelation of "*Nehmt hin mein Blut*" ("Take ye my blood"). R. tells me he wrote it down shortly before my return, with his hat and coat on, just as he was about to go out to meet me. He has had to alter the words to fit it, he says. The scene of Holy Communion will be the main scene, the core of the whole work . . . He had already told me yesterday that one must beware of having to extend a melody for the sake of the words – now today the chief passage, "*Nehmet hin mein Blut um unsrer Liebe willen, nehmet hin mein Leib und gedenket mein' ewiglich*", is there complete, in all its mildness, suffering, simplicity and exaltation. "Amfortas's sufferings are contained in it," R. says to me.'

This musical phrase, with the final words quoted by Cosima now altered to '*Nehmet hin mein Leib, auf dass ihr mein' gedenkt*', can be seen as the foundation stone of the whole work, and not only because it opens the prelude and plays a dominant part in the Communion scenes of the first and third acts: it also provides in its various parts, either directly or indirectly through inversions and other variations, most of the important motives used throughout the drama. In his book *Richard Wagner's Parsifal* (Werk-Verlag Franz Perneder, Lindau, 1951) Kurt Overhoff has revealingly traced musical connections between the Grail motive and the very different world of Klingsor and his Flower Maidens. He points out that, in contrast to the *Ring*, where they are mainly associated with persons and objects, the *Leitmotive* in *Parsifal* refer to emotional states such as innocence, compassion, greed and despair, which are common ground to all living beings, whether predominantly good or predominantly evil. The general principle underlying Wagner's deployment of them is this: diatonic modes represent purity and innocence, chromatic modes ungovernable urges and error. That diatonic themes are sometimes used in chromatic forms or vice versa, or even in mixed forms, is of course a musical reflection of the psychological tensions that constitute the drama.

Overhoff was Wieland Wagner's early teacher, and it was under the influence of his musical analyses that the composer's grandson drew up the plan for his production of *Parsifal* at Bayreuth in 1951, a production that perhaps succeeded more than any other before it in conveying the human drama underlying the work. Before starting on it, Wieland Wagner drew up a kind of blueprint, which he described as 'an attempt to express in graphic form the fundamental ideas of the work, the relationship of the characters to each other and their place in the drama.' He cast his plan in the form of a cross, with Kundry's kiss at the centre, and the contrasting and conflicting influences to which Parsifal is exposed shown on each side of the horizontal and vertical bars. One of the contrasting pairs has already been mentioned: the knights of the Grail who, unnaturally chaste, are corruptible, and the Flower Maidens who, naturally unchaste, are redeemable. Other contrasted pairs are Titurel (pure faith) and Klingsor (belief in nothing); Amfortas (the fallen spirit in Titurel's ban) and Kundry (sinful Nature in Klingsor's ban). Yet in the pursuit of redemption all commit similar mistakes: Titurel misuses the Grail to sweeten and prolong his life; Klingsor misuses the spear as a weapon to preserve his own power; Amfortas seeks salvation through forcing himself to serve the Grail as a penance, Kundry through physical abandonment to an assumed saviour. Amid these warring influences Parsifal pursues his difficult way from the innocent youth, who thoughtlessly deserts his mother Herzeleide, to the enlightened knight who returns to the motherly community of the Grail. The second act is the main battleground of the psychological drama, at its centre the kiss, which Wieland Wagner described as 'simultaneously the mystical core, climax, nadir and crisis' of Parsifal's salvation.

Though Wagner spoke of the encounter between Parsifal and Kundry in Klingsor's garden as a love scene, it is only on the surface to be seen as that, in the central situation of a seductress trying to ensnare a reluctant young man. In fact, it depicts – to use Wagner's own words – 'two worlds locked in battle for the final deliverance', a tremendous struggle of wills in the Schopenhauerian sense of the word, and it reminds us how closely Wagner's thought was akin to Schopenhauer's – unconsciously maybe in the *Ring*, but consciously in the case of *Parsifal*. Schopenhauer identifies the will with hereditary elements, and thus Kundry's attempt to seduce Parsifal occurs, not because she is in Klingsor's power, but because she is enslaved by her own erotic will, and that enables Klingsor to make use of her. As he himself mockingly tells her: '*Wohl willst du, denn du musst*' ('Verily you will, because you must') – not because *he* commands it, but because her own will demands it.

Parsifal also is not entirely immune to Kundry's attractions, otherwise he would have rejected her as totally and as self-righteously as Titurel rejected Klingsor before the drama begins. The effect of Kundry's kiss, which awakens his sympathy for Amfortas, also arouses his sympathy for Kundry: he sees her, not as evil, but as in error, as he himself has so far been and indeed still is, for he does not yet see how to put his new-found compassion, which he owes to Kundry's kiss, to any profitable use. The complicated interrelationships between good and evil, innocence and guilt, Nature and Spirit, are reflected in the music of this scene, which is built up of themes already heard, but subtly altered and juxtaposed to convey to our senses emotional disturbances far more profound than the simple situation before our eyes, and even the words, can provide on their own.

Wagner finished the vital second act on 11 October 1878, and in a letter to King Ludwig four days later he wrote: 'Well, I have thrown myself into the purgatorial melting-pot and have emerged safely from it. I know – this work too has turned out worthy of us. Now to get down without delay to the third act, which promises me blessed reward for the hard labours of the second. But first I shall have to lead it in with an orchestral prelude, in which I accompany Parsifal on his laborious and tortuous journey in search of the land of the Grail. This, however, will bring me to the Good Friday meadow – and there I shall be happy to linger.'

He composed the music of the Good Friday scene in hardly more than four weeks, after having spent almost as long to complete, with much rewriting, the mere thirty-six bars of the prelude. From that one can deduce to what extent this lyrical evocation of an atmosphere of peaceful harmony – the 'Good Friday mood' that had been the original source of inspiration for *Parsifal* – had been present musically in his mind from the very start. If one recalls his letters to Mathilde Wesendonck, one can see how the drama was subsequently constructed to lead to this visionary moment in which Wagner's perception of a divine compassion uniting the world and all its living creatures could exert its profoundest emotional effect. 'It was Schopenhauer who revealed Christianity to me,' he told Cosima, and clearly he meant that not in a doctrinal, but in a purely metaphysical sense. So overwhelming is the musical beauty with which Wagner clothed his essentially pantheistic message in this scene, consisting as it does of themes already met in the course of the drama, but now reshaped in a more tranquil and harmonious form, that one tends to pay less attention than they deserve to the actual words. These are worth recalling as they were written down in the prose sketch of 1877, where they were expressed in their simplest form: 'Parzival turns his head and gazes with gentle rapture at woods and meadow. "How beautiful the meadow seems to me today! Never have I seen it so mild and tender, stems, blossoms, flowers, all so fragrant still, so childlike in their fairness, and they spoke to me so sweetly." Gurnemanz: "That is Good Friday magic, my lord." Parzival: "Oh, the day of suffering of the All-Highest! Should not rather all creation just mourn and weep?" Gurnemanz: "You see that is not so. The sinner's remorseful tears today bedew creation. Such holy dew helps it so nobly flourish. All unreasoning creatures now rejoice in the divine Redeemer. They themselves cannot see Him on the Cross, and so they look up towards redeemed mankind, that feels itself blessed and purified by God's loving sacrifice. Each stem, each flower in the meadow becomes aware that on this day human feet will not crush it: as God took pity on mankind, now in devout homage men will spare them. Then all that blooms and is soon to die gives thanks: it is the day of innocence of Nature purified.'"

In his article *'Religion and Art'* (*'Religion und Kunst'*), written in 1879 after the completion of the orchestral score but before the final orchestration, Wagner threw further light on his conception of the problems of earthly existence and the possible ways of solving them, so different in *Parsifal* from the grim revolutionary grandeur of the *Ring*. Man, he maintained, calling Darwin and Schopenhauer to his support, was by nature a plant-eating, peace-loving species, and he had been led to meat-eating and aggression by historical circumstances. Christ's attempt to bring the world back to its proper path by example had, however, been thwarted by a power-hungry church. 'He gave up His own flesh and blood as the last and greatest atonement for all the flesh and blood sinfully slaughtered and shed, offering His disciples in their place a daily meal of wine and bread: "Such alone may ye enjoy in my remembrance."'

On the strength of Christ's example, Wagner continued, mankind should now make an attempt to regain its lost innocence, and he imagined a process of regeneration in which those who were fighting for their own particular interests – vegetarians, animal protection societies, temperance organisations and even socialists – would combine, and thus provide the basis for a new religion: 'Let us remember with the Redeemer in our hearts that it is not their actions, but their sufferings that bring the people of the past close to us and make them worthy of our remembrance, and that it is to the fallen, not to the conquering heroes that our sympathy goes out. However peaceable the condition arising from a regeneration of the human race through the agency of a quiet conscience, we shall forever continue to feel – in Nature around us, in the violence of the primitive elements, in the unalterable manifestations of the baser will operating below and beside us in sea and desert, even indeed in insects, in the worms we tread carelessly beneath our feet – the tremendous tragedy of our worldly existence, and daily we shall feel impelled to raise our eyes to the Saviour on the Cross as our ultimate sublime refuge. How happy then for us if we are enabled through our consciousness of a pure life instinct to keep our feelings for the agent of this annihilating sublimity alive, and allow ourselves to be led by an artist's depiction of the world's tragedy to a conciliatory view of human existence.'

Belief in the artist's role as admonisher and guide had always been central to Wagner's thinking and, true to his belief that it is to the fallen heroes our sympathy goes out, he had in all his previous mature works, with the obvious exception of *Die Meistersinger*, relied on the Aristotelian principle of catharsis (a purgation through the emotions of pity and terror), though he did reduce its harshness by holding out – mainly through his music – the hope of redemption for his fallen heroes or heroines after death. In *Parsifal* he at last allowed his hero to triumph in life – not quite for the first time, since he had granted the same privilege to Walther von Stolzing. The hero of *Die Meistersinger*, however, is shown in the context of a comedy, and by no stretch of the imagination can *Parsifal* be called that. A more fruitful comparison would be between Parsifal and Siegfried, both of whom we first encounter as rough and ignorant boys. At a more mature stage of his development Siegfried falls victim to the wiles of sensual love, and dies. Parsifal resists a similar temptation and lives on to carry out his mission of regeneration. He is thus not a tragic figure, and the moral lessons to be learnt from his progress cannot be conveyed to us through the emotions of pity and terror: they have to be shown. The third act of *Parsifal*, in which we see the enlightened hero at work, belongs to a tradition of which Wagner had previously made no use: that of the mystery or miracle play, in which the emphasis lies more on the message than on the figures through whom it is being conveyed.

It is in this sense that Wagner emerges more clearly as a preacher in *Parsifal* than in any other of his musical works, and it is this depiction of the hero in the act of performing his good works to the benefit of erring humanity (represented in this case by Amfortas and Kundry), in the style of the old mystery plays, that has contributed to the view that *Parsifal* is primarily a religious drama.

One must, of course, accept that the original impulse for *Parsifal* (Good Friday) was a strongly Christian one, but this should not be allowed to outweigh the evidence that, right up to the time of completing the text, Wagner saw it first and foremost as a drama of human suffering and yearning just as psychologically cogent and searching as all his previous

works. That the Christian background to the drama occupies
a more prominent place than, for example, in *Tannhäuser* or
Lohengrin, can be ascribed simply enough to the fact that
the action takes place within a Christian community. This
had to be reflected in the nature of the music, as Wagner
recognised. 'He talks about his *Parsifal*,' Cosima wrote in
her diary on 17 April 1879: 'saying it has not been possible
to avoid a certain restriction of feeling; this does not mean
that it is churchlike in tone, he says, indeed there is even
a divine wildness in it, but such affecting emotions as in
Tristan or even the *Nibelungen* would be entirely out of
place. "You will see – diminished sevenths were just not
possible."'

'Divine wildness' is a description that an orthodox Christian would probably apply not only to the music, but also
to the text of *Parsifal*, with its admixture of magic, reincarnation, pantheism and other such heresies. And it is only by
ignoring the text and confining one's attention to the musical
representation of the Last Supper that one would find any
justification for regarding the work as a religious drama in
the narrow sense of the word.

That this has nevertheless remained for so long the prevailing view of *Parsifal* is to a large extent Wagner's own
fault. His deliberate efforts to delay its stage production by
taking his time with the final orchestration were basically the
result of his reluctance to submit himself once again to all
the difficulties he had experienced during the staging of the
Ring. 'Oh, I hate the thought of all those costumes and grease
paint!' he told Cosima on 23 September 1878. 'Having created
the invisible orchestra, I now feel like inventing the invisible
theatre.' His artist's impulsion to communicate finally over-
came his protective instincts, but he then determined that
performances of his new work should be confined to his

own theatre in Bayreuth. 'Is it either possible or permissible to present in theatres such as ours,' he wrote to King Ludwig on 28 September 1880 (meaning theatres throughout Germany), 'side by side with an operatic repertoire and in front of audiences such as ours, a dramatic action in which the sublimest mysteries of the Christian religion are openly depicted?'

This apparent admission of a pious intent can, however, be interpreted as basically no more than a convenient argument to reinforce his determination, having surrendered all his other works for general performance, to keep at least this one firmly in his own hands. He invented a word to describe it – *Bühnenweihfestspiel* (literally translated, 'stage consecration festival') – that in its ambiguity further complicated the issue, for the 'consecration' can be taken to refer either to the stage or to the subject matter of the festival, and his letter to King Ludwig makes it clear that he meant the former: 'This can only mean my solitary festival theatre in Bayreuth.'

When at last, in the summer of 1882, he staged the work there, his use of the cathedral in Siena as the model for his Grail temple and his attempts to dictate at which points the audience might clap, and at which points it might not, further reinforced the impression that *Parsifal* was a sacred ceremony rather than a music drama. And so the situation remained, rigidly upheld by Cosima until the copyright expired in 1913, thirty years after Wagner's death. Though from that time onwards *Parsifal* has been staged by opera houses throughout the world, the influence of Wagner's own production has proved remarkably persistent: few producers have made serious attempts to explore the psychological insights that underlie its ritualistic surface.

Yet *Parsifal* does not stand apart from the main body of Wagner's work. It is as authentically a music drama as any of its predecessors, from which it differs essentially in one aspect only: that it shows its central figure as triumphant in life rather than in death. Its conciliatory message might be best compared with that of another enigmatic final work. In March 1882, on the eve of his presentation of *Parsifal* to the world, Wagner reread Shakespeare's *The Tempest* and remarked to Cosima that he was only now beginning entirely to understand certain beauties in its composition. *Parsifal* stands in the same relationship to *Tristan und Isolde* and the *Ring* as *The Tempest* does to *Romeo and Juliet* and *Macbeth*:

> But this rough magic
> I here abjure, and when I have required
> Some heavenly music – which even now I do –
> To work mine end upon their senses that
> This airy charm is for, I'll break my staff,
> Bury it certain fathoms in the earth,
> And deeper than did ever plummet sound
> I'll drown my book.

When Shakespeare, withdrawn from the world in Stratford-upon-Avon, put these words into Prospero's mouth, it is permissible perhaps to imagine that he was in the grip of the same valedictory mood that induced Wagner, similarly withdrawn in Bayreuth, to write to King Ludwig as he began work on the music of *Parsifal*: 'In all my living arrangements there is nothing I strive for more longingly and earnestly than to cultivate within myself all the forgetfulness and imperviousness to external things that is necessary to enable me to live from now on solely for this work. With that wish and that aim I combine a profound interest in my own survival, for, should I succeed in wresting from my vexatious fate the leisure to complete *Parsifal*, I shall indeed have celebrated my final victory over life.'